Frederick Stock

Wortfolge

Or Rules and Exercises on the Order of Words in German Sentences

Frederick Stock

Wortfolge
Or Rules and Exercises on the Order of Words in German Sentences

ISBN/EAN: 9783337157845

Printed in Europe, USA, Canada, Australia, Japan

Cover: Foto ©Thomas Meinert / pixelio.de

More available books at **www.hansebooks.com**

WORTFOLGE.

OR

RULES AND EXERCISES

ON THE

ORDER OF WORDS

IN

GERMAN SENTENCES,

WITH A VOCABULARY,

BY

FREDERICK STOCK, D. LIT., M.A. LOND.,

MEMBER OF THE COUNCIL AND FELLOW OF UNIVERSITY COLLEGE, LONDON
ASSISTANT MASTER IN MILL HILL SCHOOL.

LONDON:

GEORGE BELL AND SONS YORK STREET,
COVENT GARDEN.
1883.

· PREFACE.

IT is a common mistake in teaching composition in foreign languages to neglect rules for the order of words. Clumsy order in Greek and Latin is bad enough, but German words in false order are to a native ear and mind always intolerable and frequently unintelligible. The object of this little *Wortfolge* is to prepare the way for some such work as Dr. Buchheim's *Introduction to German Prose Composition*, by providing the pupil with certain definite rules of order such as he will never find clearly stated in ordinary elementary German exercise books. My chief authority is the twenty-third edition of Heÿse's *School Grammar*, Hannover, 1878. Eve's *Grammar* and Whitney's *Dictionary* are recommended for all cases in which the Vocabulary at the end of these Exercises is found to be deficient. The matter of the Exercises is not original; it is borrowed in a mixed form from good German and English authors.

Burton Bank, Mill Hill, N.W.

The following words should be added to the Vocabulary pages 68—82.

Find, finben, fanb, gefunben, v.i., h., acc.
German, beutſch, a. ; ein Deutſcher, ber Deutſche, n.
God, ber Gott, —es, Götter, n.
Good, gut, a.
My, mein, meine, mein, a.
Or, ober, c.c.
Our, unſer, unſere, unſer, a.
Robber, ber Räuber, —8, —n.
Snake, bie Schlange, —, —n, n.
Tame, zahm, a.
Their, ihr, ihre, ihr, a.
There, ba, bort, adv. ; sometimes es, sometimes untranslated.
To (persons), zu ; (places), nach, prep., dat. ; see Into, to bed, zu Bett.
Which, welcher, welche, welches, rel. p. and a.

N.B.—The author has adopted the German nomenclature—Subject, Copula, Predicate—in the grammatical analysis of sentences.

WORTFOLGE,

OR

RULES AND EXERCISES ON THE ORDER OF WORDS

IN

GERMAN SENTENCES.

RULES. *Group* I.

1. Every sentence in its simplest assertive form consists of a **subject**, a link or **copula**, and a **predicate**.

> *E.g.* Der Menſch iſt ſterblich.
> *Man is mortal.*

2. In German there are **three** normal positions for the **copula**, these positions depending on the function of the sentence.

3. The **copula** stands **first** in (1) **questions** expecting the answer " yes " or " no," and (2) **commands** and **wishes**.

> *E.g.* (1) Iſt der Menſch ſterblich?
> *Is man mortal?*
>
> (2) Sei gut! Sei er ein Vorbild!
> *Be good ! May he be a type !*

B

4. The **copula** stands **second** in **simple assertions**.

> *E.g.* Der Mensch ist sterblich.
> *Man is mortal.*

5. The **copula** stands **last** in **dependent** sentences
introduced by relative pronouns, such as welcher,
and by subordinating conjunctions, such as daß.
(See complete list of conjunctions, § 63).

> *E.g.* Ich weiß, daß der Mensch sterblich ist.
> *I know that man is mortal.*

6. The **position** of the **copula** is the most important point of order to be attended to in writing a
German sentence.

7. The **predicate** stands **last** in (1) **questions**,
(2) **commands** and **wishes**.

> *E.g.* Ist der Fuchs schlau?
> *Is the fox cunning?*

8. The **predicate** stands **generally last,** but
sometimes **for emphasis** **first** in **simple assertions**.

> *E.g.* Der Fuchs ist schlau, or, Schlau ist der Fuchs.
> *The fox is cunning,* or, *Cunning is the fox.*

9. The **predicate** stands **next to last** in **dependent** sentences.

> *E.g.* Ich behaupte, daß der Fuchs schlau ist.
> *I maintain that the fox is cunning.*

10. The **subject** stands **first** except in (1) questions, (2) commands and wishes, where it stands

second, and in assertions with emphatic predicate where it stands last. See previous examples.

11. Questions expecting a more particular answer than "yes" or "no" are introduced by an interrogative word, and the copula stands second.

E.g. 𝔚er ift ba? 𝔥einrid).
Who is there? *Henry.*

12. In commands and wishes the copula may stand second if in the third person.

E.g. Der eble 𝔐enfd) fei ɥülfreid) unb gut!
Let the generous man be helpful and good!

13. The copula stands first with bod) to express a strong affirmation.

E.g. 𝔍ft bod) bie 𝔖tabt wie gefeɥrt, wie ausgeftorben!
I declare the town seems swept clean, deserted!

Exercise I.

Translate into German :—
    (1) I am your friend.
    (2) Be my friend.
    (3) I believe that they are our enemies.
    (4) Foreigners are pitiable.
    (5) Germans think that Englishmen are proud.
    (6) Is the Englishman proud?
    (7) This snake is tame.
    (8) I know that you are proud of your wit.
    (9) Be gracious!
   (10) Nature is kind.

Write the following German sentences in the correct order:—

(1) Ich gehe aus, wenn das Wetter ist schön.
I go out whenever the weather is fine.

(2) Ich glücklich war, weil das grüne Gras war so erquickend.
I was happy, because the green grass was so refreshing.

(3) Er behauptete, daß die Schlange zahm sei.
He maintained that the snake was tame.

(4) Freundlich sei, da ich bin dir freundlich.
Be friendly, since I am friendly to you.

(5) Ist gütig die Natur?
Is Nature kind?

RULES. *Group* II.

14. It is convenient to regard other verbal forms besides the finite parts of the verb sein as modified forms of the copula.

15. Such are the finite parts of the verbs :—

bleiben,	*remain,*
dünken,	*seem,*
heißen,	*be called, be named,*
scheinen,	*appear,*
werden,	*become, be.*

E.g. Bleibt er gut?

Does he remain good?

Der Mensch wird alt.

Man becomes old.

Ich frage, ob er Josef heißt.

I ask whether he is called Joseph.

16. Also the finite parts of the auxiliaries :—

haben, *have,*
sein, *be,*
werden, *become, shall, will,*

in the compound verbal forms made up of these auxiliaries and the participles or infinitives of predicative verbs.

E.g. Wird er kommen?

Will he come?

Der Mann ist gestorben.

The man has died.

Wenn der Kranke geschlafen hat.

If the patient has slept.

17. Also the finite parts of the verbs of mood :—

dürfen, *be allowed,*
können, *be able, can,*
lassen, *let, cause,*
mögen, *like, may,*
müssen, *be obliged, must,*
sollen, *be destined, shall,*
wollen, *will.*

    E.g. 𝔐uß fie fterben?
    Must she die?

    Jd) will geßen.
    I will go.

    Als er mid) rufen ließ.
    When he caused me to be called.

18. Also the verbal forms of separable compound verbs. The separable particle, which always bears a strong accent, is regarded as the predicative part, and the finite verb takes the place of the copula.

    E.g. ℜommt er balb an?
    Will he arrive soon?

    𝔐ein Freund geßt mit.
    My friend will accompany me.

    𝔚eil er immer ausgeßt.
    Because he is always going out.

19. The copula and the predicate may be contained in one word. Instead of 𝔇er 𝔐enfd) ift fterblid), *Man is mortal*, we may have 𝔇er 𝔐enfd) ftirbt, *Man dies*. Whenever a single verbal form does the duty of both copula and predicate, it occupies the place of the copula.

    E.g. Stirbt ber 𝔐enfd)?
    Does man die?

    𝔇er 𝔐enfd) ftirbt.
    Man dies.

    Jd) weiß baß ber 𝔐enfd) . . . ftirbt.
    I know that man dies.

20. The negatives nid)t, nie, &c., when they simply negative the copula-containing verb, themselves take the place of the predicate, the verb taking the place of the copula.

$E.g.$ Mein Freund fommt . . . nidjt.

My friend is not coming.

21. If nid)t does not negative the copula-containing verb it stands immediately before the word which it negatives. (Cp. § 45.)

$E.g.$ Jd) habe nidjt ben großen Staatsmann fonbern ben guten Vater bewunbert.

I admired not the great politician, but the good father.

22. When the predicate is made up of more than one of these forms — negative, separable particle, past participle, infinitive—the order of the parts of the predicate between themselves is that just enumerated, viz. negative, particle, participle, infinitive.

$E.g.$ Er wirb nidjt ausgegangen fein.

23. Examine the details of the subjoined scheme :—

Questions.

Copula.	Subject.	Modifications.	Predicate.
Jft	ber Menfd)	,,	fterblid) ?
Bleibt	ber Menfd)	,,	fterblid) ?
Hat	ber Kranfe	,,	gefdjlafen ?
Kann	ber Kranfe	,,	fdjlafen ?
Kommt	ber König	,,	an ?
Kommt	ber König	,,	nidjt ?

Assertions.

Subject.	Copula.	Modifications.	Predicate.
Der Menſch	iſt	„	ſterblich.
Der Menſch	bleibt	„	ſterblich.
Der Kranke	hat	„	geſchlafen.
Der Kranke	kann	„	ſchlafen.
Der König	kommt	„	an.
Der König	kommt	„	nicht.

Dependent on Ich weiß daß, I know that.

Subject.	Modifications.	Predicate.	Copula.
Der Menſch	„	ſterblich	iſt.
Der Menſch	„	ſterblich	bleibt.
Der Kranke	„	geſchlafen	hat.
Der Kranke	„	ſchlafen	kann.
Der König	„	an	kommt.
Der König	„	nicht	kommt.

Exercise II. (partly from Lessing).

Translate :—

(1) We remain friends.

(2) He is called John.

(3) I say that he is called John.

(4) She believes that he wishes to go away.

(5) I declare I have never seen the market and the streets so deserted.

(6) I wished to reply.

(7) We know that the streets of Constantinople are dirty.

(8) These children remain naughty.

(9) We saw the king when we were in Berlin.

(10) I think that the answer is easy.

Write in correct order :—

(1) Willst du, daß ich dich so umbilden soll?
Do you wish me to transform you thus?

(2) Die Nachtigall und der Pfau Freunde wurden.
The nightingale and the peacock were friends.

(3) Ein Schäfer hatte verloren durch eine grausame Seuche seine ganze Heerde.
A shepherd had lost his entire flock by a fell pestilence.

(4) Ich möchte weinen blutige Thränen!
I could weep tears of blood.

(5) Der Esel zu dem Aesopus sprach: Wenn du bringst wieder ein Geschichtchen von mir aus, so laß mich etwas recht Vernünftiges und Sinnreiches sagen.
The ass said to Æsop: When you produce another story about me, make me say something downright witty and clever.

RULES. *Group* III.

24. Verbs may require completion, may govern direct and indirect objects. Verbs may also be modified by adverbs and by adjects (prepositions with their governed nouns). In the order of these words

there is more variety, yet not capricious variety.
The general principle underlying the following special
rules is that words of **less importance** and of less
emphasis **precede** those of greater importance and
of greater emphasis.

25. The **Dative precedes** the **Accusative** except
in the case of pronouns of the third person. Between
pronouns of the third person the accusative precedes
the dative. If the question of precedence lies between pronouns of the third person, whether dative
or accusative, and nouns, the pronouns generally
stand first because of their lighter emphasis.

E.g. Mein Vater hat **dem Manne das Buch** gegeben.
My father has given the man the book.

Mein Vater hat **es ihm** gegeben.
My father has given it to him.

Mein Vater hat **ihm das Buch** gegeben.
My father has given him the book.

Mein Vater hat **es dem Manne** gegeben.
My father has given it to the man.

26. The personal pronouns of the first and second
persons follow generally the rule given for pronouns
of the third person, but perhaps themselves more
frequently bear a heavier accentuation.

27. The **reflexive pronoun** sich, dative and accusative, stands **before** all other completions and
extensions of the predicate. (Cp. § 53, end.)

28. The **Genitive** usually **follows** the **Accusative**, and always when the genitive belongs to the predicate and is not an attribute of the accusative noun.

E.g. Wir beschuldigen den Mann des Diebstahls.
We accuse the man of theft.

29. The **Adverb** may stand either

(1) **before** the Dative,

or, (2) **between** the Dative and Accusative,

or, (3) **after** the Accusative.

E.g. Ich habe **gestern** meinem Sohne das Buch gegeben.
I gave my son the book yesterday.

or, Ich habe meinem Sohne **gestern** das Buch gegeben.

or, Ich habe es ihm **gestern** gegeben.

The adverb rarely stands after the accusative unless both dative and accusative are words of light accent.

30. The **Adject** (preposition with case) if it modifies the predicate, and is not an enlargement of the subject or object, stands immediately before the predicate when the predicate is separated from the copula.

E.g. Ich habe ihm den Brief zum Lesen gegeben.
I gave him the letter to read.

31. When the predicate and copula are contained in one verbal form this adverbial adject in simple assertions stands last.

E.g. Ich gab ihm den Brief zum Lesen.
I gave him the letter to read.

32. If the predicate is an adjective, the adverbial adject may stand either before or after the adjective.

E.g. Er ift an Gelbe arm ; or, Er ift arm an Gelbe.
He is poor in pocket.

33. If **Adverbs** of more than one class occur, the adverb of **time** should **precede** the adverb of **place**, and the adverb of **place** should **precede** the adverb of **manner**.

E.g. Er war geftern hier gefährlich frant.
He was dangerously ill here yesterday.

34. If several **adverbs** of the **same class** occur, the **less special** and emphatic should **precede** the **more special** and emphatic.

E.g. Hier im Garten,   Heute früh.
Here in the garden, Early this morning.

35. An adverbial adject is frequently not to be distinguished from an adverb of time, place, degree, or manner.

Exercise III. (partly from Lessing).

Translate into German :—

(1) The spray falls down again.

(2) If you are Solomon, how can you ask ?

(3) The fox lay on his death-bed at last.

(4) I wrote a letter when I arrived here in May.

(5) The ant always works industriously.

(6) The wolf took-advantage-of (sich zu Nutze machen) the circumstance.

(7) Speak if you understand it.

(8) I have given you these nuts to crack (zum Knacken).

(9) The trees were almost leafless in many places in May.

(10) We shall go from here at the end of the summer.

Write in correct order :—

(1) Der Rabe bemerkte, daß der Adler brütete über seinen Eiern ganze dreißig Tage.

The raven noticed that the eagle sat on her eggs for thirty whole days.

(2) Ich gebe gern ihm es.

I gladly give it to him.

(3) Gehe hin zur Ameise noch einmal.

Go once more to the ant.

(4) Der Arzt hat behandelt ihn in dem Spital mit großer Sorgfalt während seiner Krankheit.

The physician treated him with great care during his illness in the hospital.

(5) Der König war damals in Wien.

The king was at that time in Vienna.

RULES. *Group* IV.

36. A very **characteristic** peculiarity of the German language is to be found in its accurate **word-grouping.**

An **assertion** respecting a subject is grouped or grasped into unity by the **bracketing** force of **copula** and **predicate,** the copula standing next after the subject and the predicate at the extreme end.

E.g. Der Menſch iſt immer unb überall ſterblich.
Man is mortal always and everywhere.

37. In **subordinate** sentences we have also found a very effectual grouping produced by the shifting of the copula to the end of the sentence. The **bracketing** is here effected by the introductory **conjunction** or **relative pronoun** at the commencement and by the **copula** at the close of such sentences.

E.g. Ich weiß, daß der Menſch jetzt in England ſterblich iſt.
I know that man is mortal now in England.

38. A **similar grouping** is effected by the position of the **enlargements** of the subject and object in a sentence. Qualifying enlargements of the subject and object generally **precede** the word qualified.

39. The **attributive** adjective **precedes** the noun.

E.g. Guter Knabe.
Good buy.

40. **Demonstrative** adjectives precede **numeral** adjectives, **numeral** adjectives **precede qualitative** adjectives, and generally adjectives of **less special** meaning **precede** those of **more special** meaning.

E.g. Der gute Knabe. Diese drei guten Männer.

The good boy. *These three good men.*

41. If the qualitative adjective is itself modified by an adverb or by an immediately dependent substantive, the **adverb** or **dependent substantive** precedes the **adjective**.

E.g. Ein sehr guter Knabe.
A very good boy.

Ein des Rechtes kundiger Mann.
A man skilled in the law.

42. If a **qualitative adjective** is **modified** by **both** a dependent **substantive** and an **adverb,** the **adverb follows** the **substantive.**

E.g. Ein der deutschen Sprache vollkommen kundiger Frember.

A foreigner perfectly well acquainted with the German language.

43. Under this rule may be taken the favourite German contracted sentences.

E.g. Der von allen sehr geliebte Staatsmann.
The statesman who is greatly beloved by all.

44. Adverbs are occasionally used as shortened adjective sentences, and then follow the noun.

E.g. Der Mann hier.   Die Bäume dort.

The man here.   *The trees yonder.*

45. **Adverbs** of degree and mood, if especially **calling attention** to a **substantive**, immediately **precede** the **substantive**.

E.g. Vorzüglich Sokrates hat die Mäßigung empfohlen.

Socrates especially has recommended temperance.

Auch du hast es gesagt.

Thou too didst say so.

Nicht ich habe es gethan.

It was not I that did it.   (Cp. §§ 20, 21.)

46. A preposition with its case when equivalent to an adjective, that is to say an **adjectival adject**, often **follows** the **noun** qualified.

E.g. Ein Mann von Blut und Eisen.

A man of blood and iron.

47. Dependent **genitives** generally **follow** the **noun** on which they depend, but sometimes genitives, especially of Proper Names without the article, precede the noun on which they depend.   (Cp. § 28.)

E.g. Der Herr des Hauses.   Heinrichs Regierung.

The master of the house. Henry's reign.

48. In poetry the governed genitive with the article often precedes the governing noun, which always stands without any article.

E.g. Der Mutter liebes Kind.

The mother's dear child.

Exercise IV. (partly from Kuno Fischer).

Translate into German :—

(1) Schiller's works are praised by all.

(2) This author has written several very interesting books.

(3) A fox once found the hollow gaping mask of an actor.

(4) This medicine, (which is) very salutary for the patient, has been given to me by a well known doctor.

(5) Al Hafi, with his predilection for the Parsees, with his longing for the teachers by the Ganges, is hardly a character conformable to Islam.

(6) The main thing in Lessing's *Nathan* is not the action but the idea.

(7) The root of his character is just this natural nobility of his disposition.

(8) Sittah will make an excellent aunt.

(9) This man, well acquainted with all European languages, acquired a high rank among diplomatists.

(10) Experience of the world may make us witty and clever.

C

Write in correct order :—

(1) Die Bemerkung, welche liegt hier zum Grunde,
daß der Schmerz in dem Gesichte des Laokoon mit
derjenigen Wuth sich nicht zeige, welche man
sollte bei der Heftigkeit desselben vermuthen,
vollkommen richtig ist.

This fundamental observation, that pain is not
exhibited in the features of Laokoon with that
passionate madness which one might expect
from the violence of the pain, is perfectly
just.

(2) Der König und die Königin, mit ihren sechs
Brüdern, lebten lange Jahre in Glück und
Frieden.

The king and the queen, with their six brothers,
lived many a long year in happiness and
peace.

(3) Die Größe der moralischen Kraft sich durch die
Größe des Widerstandes mißt, den sie findet
und besiegt.

The amount of moral force is measured by the
amount of resistance which it meets with and
overpowers.

(4) Komme hierher früh morgen.

Come here to-morrow morning.

(5) Die menschlichen Leidenschaften maßlos sind.

Human passions are boundless.

RULES. *Group* V.

49. Genug always follows the adjective or adverb which it modifies.

> *E.g.* Er ift jung genug.
> *He is young enough.*

50. Voll, when it governs a substantive, follows the substantive which it qualifies and remains unchanged.

> *E.g.* Eine Hand voll Geld.
> *A hand full of money.*

51. The accusative of space or time passed over is placed before the adjective which it modifies.

> *E.g.* Zwei Ellen lang.
> *Two yards long.*
>
> Ein zwölf Jahre alter Knabe.
> *A boy twelve years old.*

52. Read over the previous rules and then the following example :—

Diefer fehr ftolze Vater hat heute vormittag hier in diefem nieblichen Zimmerchen feinem guten von Allen hoch gepriefenen Sohne diefes außerordentlich unterhaltende Buch zum Lefen gegeben.

This very proud father this morning, in this pretty little room here, gave his good son, who is highly praised by every one, this extraordinarily interesting book to read.

Exercise V. (from Lessing).

Translate into German :—

The furious north wind had proved his strength one stormy night on a lofty oak. It lay now at-full-length (geſtreďt), and a multitude of low bushes lay smashed under it. A fox, who had his hole not far from-the-place (baďon), saw the oak the next morning and said, " What a tree! I declare I should never have thought it would-have-been (subj. plupf.) so great."

Write in correct order :—

Jď möďte wiſſen woýl, ob der Rabe ýat Antýeil an den Opfern, weil er iſt ein propýetiſďer Vogel, oder ob man ýält iýn für einen propýetiſďen Vogel, weil er iſt genug freď, die Opfer mit den Göttern zu týeilen. (Do not alter the order of the last seven words).

I should be glad to know whether the raven has a share in the sacrifices because he is a prophetic bird, or whether he is considered to be a prophetic bird because he is impudent enough to share the sacrifices with the gods.

RULES. *Group* VI.

53. For the sake of **emphasis** or **variety** instead of the subject any one of the following—object, direct or indirect, **adverb** or **adject**—may stand **first** in a categorical or assertive sentence.

In this case the **copula** or copula-containing verb

still maintains its place as the **second** member of the sentence, and the **subject** is **shifted** to the **third** place or even to the **fourth** place, if there is a **reflexive** pronoun or other **word** of **light** accentuation claiming the **third** place.

E.g. Die Mutter hat geſtern dem Mädchen ein Feder= meſſer geliehen.

The mother lent the girl a penknife yesterday.

may be written :—

Geſtern hat die Mutter dem Mädchen ein Federmeſſer geliehen.

or, Dem Mädchen hat die Mutter geſtern ein Feder= meſſer geliehen.

or, Ein Federmeſſer hat die Mutter geſtern dem Mädchen geliehen.

In the same way the sentence :—

Der Menſch widmete ſich in vergangenen Zeiten der Pflege der Kranken nicht.

Man did not in former times devote himself to the nursing of the sick.

may be expressed by :—

In vergangenen Zeiten widmete ſich der Menſch der Pflege der Kranken nicht.

54. In an **infinitive sentence** with zu the zu immediately precedes the infinitive, which always stands last. Such a sentence is frequently intro-

duced by um or some other preposition, so that here again is an instance of German accurate **word-grouping** or bracketing.

E.g. Um hier in diesem Garten zu sterben.

In order to die here in this garden.

Ohne so viel zu sagen.

Without saying as much.

Exercise VI. (from Grimm and Kuno Fischer).

(1) A father once caused his three sons to come before him.

(2) One summer morning a little tailor sat on his table at the window.

(3) In this wood two giants lived.

(4) In walking I am not idle.

(5) At evening Cinderella was obliged to lie in the ashes near the hearth.

(6) On the third day Cinderella went again to her mother's grave.

(7) No sacred lore can save the hypocrite.

(8) In this dramatic picture of religious characters even the complete opposite of true religion may not be absent.

(9) The Crusades form an important crisis in the faith of the Christian world.

(10) In the first scene Faust appears at his study-table.

Write in correct order:—

(1) Eines Tages ein Königssohn gerieth in einen großen Wald.
One day a king's son came into a great forest.

(2) Bei Anbruch der Nacht sie fanden ein Wirthshaus.
At nightfall they found an inn.

(3) Der Diener gab dem Wirth den Raben, den er sollte bereiten zum Abendessen.
The servant gave the landlord the raven, which he was to prepare for their supper.

(4) Dem Raben hatte sich das Gift von dem Pferde= fleisch mitgetheilt.
The raven had been infected with the poison of the horseflesh.

(5) Am oberen Ende des Orts ein Wegweiser steht.
At the upper end of the village stands a sign post.

RULES. *Group* VII.

55. **Instead** of a simple **adverb** or adverbial expression we may have an adverbial **sentence**, that is, a sentence equivalent to an adverb. Such a sentence is grouped as a unity by its introductory conjunction and its closing copula or finite verb form.

E.g. Als ich in Berlin war = damals.
When I was in Berlin = then.

56. If we had a sentence commencing with damals, the copula or copula-containing finite verb would have to follow next; and so in a **complex sentence,** if the adverbial subordinate sentence stands first, the copula of the principal sentence follows immediately.

E.g. Als ich in Berlin war, sah ich ben König von Preußen.

When I was in Berlin, I saw the King of Prussia.

57. So **instead** of a noun we may have a **noun-sentence,** that is, a sentence equivalent to a noun, as either subject or object to the verb of the principal sentence.

E.g. Diese Thatsache weiß Jebermann.

This fact every one knows.

Instead of diese Thatsache we may have the sentence:—

Daß diese Geschichte wahr ist.

That this history is true.

and the complex sentence will stand thus:—

Daß diese Geschichte wahr ist, weiß Jebermann.

Every one knows that this history is true.

Ob der Homer bie Iliabe schrieb, ist nicht sicher.

It is not certain whether Homer wrote the Iliad.

58. **Adjective sentences,** that is, sentences equivalent to adjectives, generally stand **after** the noun which they qualify, and are themselves, too, like

adverb and noun sentences accurately grouped by their introductory relative and their closing verbal form. (Cp. Supplementary Rules.)

E.g. Der Knabe, welcher rechtschaffen und ehrlich ist, braucht nichts zu fürchten.

The boy, who is upright and honourable, needs fear nothing.

59. **In complex sentences in German the subordinate noun and adverb sentences are favourites for the first place.**

60. Of course both noun sentences and adverb sentences may, and frequently do, stand in the other places open to a simple noun or simple adverb. (Cp. § 29.)

E.g. Jedermann weiß, daß diese Geschichte wahr ist. Ich sah, als ich in Berlin war, den König von Preußen.

Exercise VII. (partly from Grimm).

(1) As they did not return, their father became impatient.

(2) One day her grandmother presented her a little hood of red velvet, and because the hood suited her so well, she was always called Little Red Riding Hood.

(3) When Little Red Riding Hood came into the wood, a wolf met her.

(4) When the wolf had appeased his hunger, he got into bed again. (Ger., laid himself to bed again.)

(5) They could not reach Bremen in one day, and came at evening into a wood, where they thought of passing (Ger., wished to pass) the night.

(6) While I was still in London, my stepbrother's wife died.

(7) She was really a pious, honest woman who offended nobody.

(8) Her one failing she inherited from her mother.

(9) But even this failing was to be excused. (Ger., to excuse.)

(10) Because she did it not from vanity but from habit.

Write in correct order :—

(1) Napoleon mit Sehnsucht erwartete die Nacht, die sollte erretten seine noch übrigen hartbebräng= ten Haufen aus der Hand der ungestümen Feinde.

Napoleon anxiously awaited the night which was to rescue his still remaining hard pressed troops from the hand of the impetuous enemy.

(2) Eine Stiftung neuer Art und eigener Gattung ist diese spanische Inquisition, die findet kein Vor= bild im ganzen Laufe der Zeiten, und steht zu vergleichen mit keinem geistlichen, keinem weltlichen Tribunal.

An establishment of a new kind and of a peculiar species is this Spanish Inquisition,

*which has no precedent in the whole course of
history, and is comparable to no ecclesiastical
and no civil tribunal.*

(3) Auf der andern Seite des Waldes ein Theil
desselben Stammes wohnt.

*On the other side of the forest dwells a section of
the same tribe.*

(4) Als Jupiter feierte das Fest seiner Vermählung,
Juno vermißte das Schaf.

*When Jupiter was celebrating the festival of his
marriage, Juno missed the sheep.*

(5) Die Ziegen baten den Zeus zu geben Hörner
ihnen auch.

The goats asked Zeus to give them also horns.

RULES. *Group* VIII.

61. The rules for the order of words after conjunctions are more complicated. We have to make a
somewhat illogical division into **Coordinating, Subordinating**, and **Adverbial** conjunctions.

62. **Coordinating** conjunctions do **not** in any
way **affect** the **order** of the sentence introduced by
them. They are :—

aber,	*but, moreover,*
allein,	*but, only, yet,*
denn,	*for,*

ſonbern, *but* (after negatives),
ober,   *or*,
unb,   *and*.

E.g. Allein ber Menſch iſt ſterblich.
But man is mortal.

Denn mit Göttern ſoll ſich nicht meſſen
Irgenb ein Menſch.—GOETHE.
For with gods must no mere man
Make trial of strength.

63. **Subordinating** conjunctions **shift** the co**pula**
or copula-containing verb to the **end** of the sentence
introduced by them. Most of these conjunctions are
relative adverbs.

They are:—

als,	*when, as,*
bevor,	*before,*
bis,	*until,*
ba,	*since, as,*
bafern,	*if,*
bamit,	*in order that,*
baß,	*that,*
ehe,	*before,*
falls,	*in case that,*
je mehr,	*the more,*
je nachbem,	*according as,*
inbem,	*while, as,*
inſofern, inſoweit, in wie fern, in wie weit,	} *as far as,*
nachbem,	*after,*

ob,	*if, whether,*
obgleich, obschon, obwohl, ob= zwar,	*although,*
seitdem,	*since,*
so,	*however, if,*
sofern, soweit,	*as far as,*
während,	*whilst,*
warum, weßhalb, weßwegen,	*why,*
wann,	*when,*
weil,	*because,*
wenn,	*when, whenever, if,*
wenngleich, wennschon, wenn auch,	*although,*
wie,	*as,*
wie fern, wie weit,	*as far as,*
wie auch,	*however,*
wie wohl,	*although,*
wo,	*where,*
wofern,	*if.*

E.g. Da der Mensch sterblich ist.
Since man is mortal.

64. **Adverbial conjunctions attract** the **copula.**
The **copula** or copula-containing verb stands **next**
after the adverbial **conjunction.** Almost any
demonstrative adverb may serve as an adverbial
conjunction, but some of the more common adverbial
conjunctions are subjoined.

also,	*thus, therefore, then,*
auch,	*also,*

außerdem,	besides,
daher,	therefore,
damit,	therewith,
dann, alsdann,	then, after that,
darauf,	thereupon,
darum, deßwegen, deßhalb,	therefore,
demnach,	consequently,
dennoch,	still, yet,
dessenungeachtet, nichtsdesto= weniger,	} nevertheless,
desto mehr,	the more,
einerseits, andrerseits,	{ on the one side, on the other side,
endlich,	at last,
ferner,	further, moreover,
folglich,	consequently,
gleichwohl,	however,
hernach, nachher,	afterwards,
hingegen, dagegen,	on the other hand,
indessen, indeß,	in the meantime,
insofern, insoweit,	so far, thus far,
kaum,	hardly,
mithin,	therefore,
noch,	yet, still,
so,	thus, so,
sonst,	else, otherwise,
theils—theils,	partly—partly,
übrigens,	however,
überdies,	moreover, besides,
unterdessen,	meanwhile,

vielmehr,	*rather,*
wohl,	*indeed, perhaps,*
zudem,	*moreover, besides,*
zwar,	*indeed, to be sure.*

E.g. Nichts destoweniger ist der Mensch sterblich.
Nevertheless man is mortal.

65. The **following adverbial** conjunctions are used as **coordinating** conjunctions when serving as a kind of **interjection.**

doch,	*still, though,*
jedoch,	*still, though,*
indessen	*however,*
nun,	*now,*
freilich,	*to be sure, certainly,*
wahrlich,	*really.*

E.g. Wahrlich du hast Unrecht.
Really you are wrong.

66. The **following adverbial** conjunctions are used as **coordinating** conjunctions not affecting the order of the sentence introduced by them, when they **refer** more particularly to the **subject** or **object** which will immediately follow them. (Cp. §§ 21, 45.)

auch,	*also, too,*
entweder,	*either,*
kaum,	*scarcely, hardly,*
nicht allein, nicht bloß, nicht nur—sondern auch,	} *not only—but also,*
nur,	*only,*

ſchon,	*already,*
ſelbſt,	*even,*
ſogar,	*indeed,*
ſowohl—als (auch),	*both—and,*
weder—noch,	*neither—nor.*

E.g. Nur eins fehlt noch.
Only one thing is still wanting.

67. Carefully notice the difference between wie? *how?* and wie, *as, how;* between wann? *when?* and wann, *when* (introducing a dependent question); and notice the same difference with warum, weßwegen, weßhalb.

68. Notice the order in the following sentence with je mehr—deſto:—

Je mehr der Vorrath ſchmolz, deſto (or um ſo, or je) ſchrecklicher wuchs der Hunger.—SCHILLER.

The more the provisions diminished, the more terribly the famine increased.

Exercise VIII. (from Grimm).

(1) The louder he cried, the more vigorously did the cudgel beat the time to-his-cries (ihm dazu) on his back.

(2) The beast was so big and strong that no one ventured into the neighbourhood of the wood in which it lived (hauſen).

(3) The box did not sink, but swam like a little boat.

(4) Then the robbers let the boy lie peacefully on the bench until the following morning; and when he had awakened they gave him the letter and showed him the right way.

(5) The golden hairs I will certainly bring; I am not afraid of the giant.

(6) At (mit) sunrise she set-out (sich auf ben Weg machen), and walked the whole day until it became night.

(7) The king ate nothing and drank nothing during (all) this time, but God sustained him.

(8) Thereupon the angel went into the room where the queen sat with her son.

(9) In Switzerland (there) once lived an old count who had only one single son, and this (son) was stupid and could learn nothing.

(10) When he came back, his father asked again: " My son, what have you learned?"

Write in correct order :—

(1) Ich weiß Alles, er antwortete.

I know everything, he answered.

(2) Ein Müller war nach und nach gerathen in Armuth, und nichts mehr als seine Mühle und einen großen Apfelbaum dahinter hatte.

A miller had gradually fallen into poverty, and had nothing left except his mill and a large apple-tree behind it.

(3)、 Die Müllerstochter war ein schönes und frommes Mädchen, und lebte die drei Jahre in Gottes= furcht und ohne Sünde.

The miller's daughter was a good and beautiful girl, and spent these three years in innocence and in the fear of God.

(4) Ich will gehen, so weit der Himmel ist blau, und nicht essen und nicht trinken, bis ich habe wieder gefunden meine liebe Frau und mein Kind.

I will go as far as the blue heaven reaches, and will eat and drink nothing until I have found my dear wife and child again.

(5) Darauf er mußte singen eine Messe und wußte kein Wort davon, aber die zwei Tauben stets saßen auf seinen Schultern und sagten ihm Alles ins Ohr.

Afterwards he was obliged to sing a mass and he did not know a word of it, but the two doves perched on his shoulders and whispered it all to him.

RULES. *Group* IX.

69. In **commands** and **wishes** in the **third person** it is usual to **express** the **subject** or **object,** which follows the copula or copula-containing verb, also **before** the **copula** in the general form es. This es may be regarded as in **apposition** to the following subject or object.

E.g. Es scheine die Sonne!
May it shine! viz. the sun.
May the sun shine!

Es fürchte die Götter das Menschengeschlecht.
Let mankind fear the gods.—GOETHE.

70. **This order** of words is also **very common**
in simple categorical or **assertive** sentences.

E.g. Es leuchtet die Sonne.
The sun is bright.

Es sperren die Riesen den einsamen Weg.
Giants block the lonely road.

Es hatte ein Mann einen Esel.
A man had an ass.

Es war einmal eine arme Frau.
There was once a poor woman.

71. It is still more frequent to anticipate a subject
or object noun sentence by this appositional es.

E.g. Es ist wahr, daß der Mensch sterblich ist.
It is true, that man is mortal.

Es weiß ein Jeder, daß du eifersüchtig bist.
Every one knows that you are jealous.

72. A **similar kind** of apposition or repetition
is found in the use of so **after** adverb sentences.
The so is in **apposition** to the **adverb sentence.**

E.g. Als ich in Berlin war, so sah ich ben König von Preußen.

When I was in Berlin, I saw the King of Prussia.

73. Instead of so, da may be used.

E.g. Wenn wir das Kind hierher schicken, Trinken zu zapfen, da kann ihm ja die Kreuzhacke den Kopf zer= schlagen.—GRIMM.

If we send the child here to draw liquor, to be sure the hatchet may dash his brains out.

74. The appositional es, so, and da, remain un-expressed in English.

75. Es is still more obviously used in **apposition** to object infinitive sentences.

E.g. Er hatte es gewagt, sich heimlich aufzumachen.

He had ventured to go in secret.

76. Es may also stand in apposition to an ordinary object noun sentence **without affecting** the **order** of the principal sentence (cp. § 71).

E.g. Ich leide es nicht, daß ihr sie töbtet.—GRIMM.

I will not allow you to kill them.

77. Another case of somewhat complicated appo-sition is of great importance in the idiomatic render-ing of the English gerund when governed by a preposition. The **demonstrative part** of such

words as **baran, baburch, bavon,** stands in apposition to a following noun sentence.

E.g. Der arme Bruber nährte sich bavon, daß er Bejen band.

The poor brother got his living by making brooms.

Der König war lange Zeit nicht zu tröjten, und dachte nicht baran, eine zweite Frau zu nehmen.

The king was long inconsolable, and never thought of taking a second wife.

Exercise IX. (from Grimm).

Translate into German :—

(1) There was once a poor peasant who had a beautiful daughter.

(2) If one set it up and said, " Little table, be spread " (cover thyself), the good little table was at once covered with a clean little cloth.

(3) However, it did not speak a word, but led them to a richly garnished table, and when they had eaten and drunk, it conducted every one into his own sleeping room.

(4) " Yes," answered the wife with-a-sigh (Ger., and sighed), " if it were only a little child, I would be contented."

(5) When the two strange men caught sight of Tom Thumb, they did not know what to-say (Ger., they should say) for (vor) astonishment.

(6) If they have not left off, they are dancing still.

(7) A shoemaker had become so poor without-fault-of-his-own (ohne seine Schuld), that at last nothing was left him but leather for a single pair of shoes.

(8) With-the-shoemaker (dat.) it went well as long as he lived.

(9) The coverlets were embroidered with gold, the cradle was of ivory, the bath-tub of gold.

(10) As often as she looked at him or thought of him, she experienced a terrible-fear (Grauen) in her heart.

Write in correct order :—

(1) Daumesdick immer kroch weiter zurück, und da es bald ward ganz dunkel, so sie mußten mit Aerger und mit leerem Beutel wandern heim wieder.

Tom Thumb crept further and further back, and as it soon became quite dark they were obliged to go home again in vexation without him.

(2) „Ach nein," die Katze antwortete, „er nur einen Schwanz hat." „So ich will ihn haben nicht."

“Ah no,” answered the cat, “he has only one tail.” “ Then I will not have him.”

(3) Weil er hatte ein gutes Gewissen, so legte er sich ruhig zu Bett, befahl sich dem lieben Gott und einschlief.

As he had a good conscience, he got quietly into bed, committed himself to God's keeping, and fell asleep.

(4) Als es war Mitternacht, da kamen zwei kleine niebliche nackte Männlein, sich setzten vor des Schusters Tisch, nahmen alle zugeschnittene Arbeit zu sich, und anfiengen mit ihren Finger= lein so behend und schnell zu stechen, zu nähen, zu klopfen, daß der Schuster konnte vor Ver= wunderung nicht die Augen abwenden.

At midnight there came two dear little naked mannikins, who sat down before the shoemaker's table, took in hand all the work already cut out, and with their little fingers began to prick, sew, and hammer so cleverly and quickly, that the shoemaker could not take his eyes off them for astonishment.

RULES. *Group* X.

78. The order of verbal forms among themselves in the active voice in assertive and dependent sentences is the following :—

ASSERTIVE.	DEPENDENT.
Ich schreibe das,	was ich schreibe.
I write that	*which I write.*
Ich habe das geschrieben,	was ich geschrieben habe.
I have written that	*which I have written.*

Assertive.	Dependent.
Ich hatte das geschrieben,	was ich geschrieben hatte.
I had written that	*which I had written.*
Ich werde das schreiben,	was ich schreiben werde.
I shall write that	*which I shall write.*
Ich würde das schreiben,	was ich schreiben würde.
I should write that	*which I should write.*
Ich werde das geschrieben haben,	was ich geschrieben haben werde.
I shall have written that	*which I shall have written.*
Ich würde das geschrieben haben,	was ich geschrieben haben würde,
or, Ich hätte das geschrieben,	*or,* was ich geschrieben hätte.
I should have written that	*which I should have written*

Notice that **was** is **relative** to the **vague** antecedent **das**.

79. Difficulties of order arise when we come to the verbs of mood. Instead of ich, habe thun gewollt the German idiom is ich habe thun wollen, *I have desired to do*, and it is to be carefully noted that this order, ich habe thun wollen, is retained in relative and other dependent sentences.

E.g. Ich habe thun wollen, was ich habe thun wollen.

I have desired to do what I have desired to do.

80. When there are two or more apparent infinitives in the compound verbal expression, the **finite verb** or copula stands **before** these infinitive forms **even** in relative and other dependent sentences.

E.g. Augenblidlich war es mit Speisen besetzt, so gut wie sie der Wirth nicht hätte herbeischaffen können.

GRIMM.

Immediately it was covered with better kinds of food than the landlord could have procured.

81. The rule may be stated in this form : When an infinitive stands for a past participle, it allows nothing to stand after it in its own sentence, and it is itself immediately preceded by its dependent infinitive.

82. This order is sometimes imitated (1) when the two infinitive forms are both real infinitives, and (2) when one is a real participle followed by an infinitive.

E.g. (1) Doch hoffte man, die Stadt wenigstens so lange hinzuhalten, bis man das Getreide würde einernten können.—SCHILLER.

Still they hoped to hold the town, at any rate until the corn harvest might be got in.

(2) Denn ein wohlausgedachter Plan, wenn er ausgeführt dasteht, läßt alles vergessen was die Mittel, um zu diesem Zweck zu gelangen, Unbequemes mögen gehabt haben.—GOETHE.

For whenever a well matured plan has been carried to completion, it makes us forget all the discomforts which may have been occasioned by the means adopted in order to arrive at this end.

83. The infinitive of the auxiliary **haben** is made to **precede** the other **infinitive forms** when the last of them is equivalent to a **past participle**.

E.g. Jhr werdet mich **haben** ermorden laſſen **wollen**.
You will have wanted to get me murdered.

Cp. Der Mann, welchen ich **habe** erretten laſſen **wollen**.
The man whom I wished to get rescued.

Exercise X. (from Grimm).

(1) "Servant!" answered the beggar, "you must yourself do what you want to get done."

(2) You ought to have cut the stick in two.

(3) The ring was so beautiful that no goldsmith on earth could have made it.

(4) "Ah, dear father," the child answered, "they are gone (fort) and have left me alone."

(5) Then she fell on his neck (einem um den Hals fallen).

(6) The child showed him the feathers which they had let fall in the courtyard, and which she had picked up.

(7) Then her envious heart had rest, as far as an envious heart can have rest.

(8) In this disguise she went over the seven mountains to the seven dwarfs.

(9) Because the child was so beautiful, the huntsman had pity.

(10) The proposal pleased the dog, and as it was planned so it was carried-out (ausgeführt).

Write in correct order:—

(1) Sie ließ holen gleich ihre große Schachtel und gab ihm daraus einen Ring, der glänzte von Edelsteinen.

She immediately sent for her great box, and from it gave him a ring which glittered with precious stones.

(2) Der König merkte, daß viele harte Thaler fehlten, konnte aber nicht begreifen, wer sie sollte gestohlen haben.

The king noticed that many silver dollars were wanting, but could not conceive who should have stolen them.

(3) Der Tod packte ihn mit seiner eiskalten Hand so hart, daß er nicht konnte widerstehen.

Death grasped him so hard with his icy hand that he could not resist.

(4) Wenn Seine Majestät machten einen Spaziergang, Alles floh vor ihm aus dem Wege, als ob ein Tiger wäre losgebrochen aus dem Käfig.

*When His Majesty took a walk, every human being fled before him, as if a tiger had broken loose from a menagerie.—*MACAULAY.

(5) Der Keſſel, welchen ich aufſetzen müſſen habe, iſt von Eiſen.

The caldron, which I have been obliged to put on the fire, is made of iron.

RULES. *Group* XI.

84. The order of passive compound verbal forms closely resembles that of the active forms. .

ASSERTIVE.	DEPENDENT.
Er wird von demjenigen getabelt,	von welchem er getabelt wird.
He is blamed by the man	*by whom he is blamed.*
Er wurde von demjenigen getabelt,	von welchem er getabelt wurde.
He was blamed by the man	*by whom he was blamed.*
Er wird von demjenigen getabelt werden,	von welchem er getabelt werden wird.
	or, von welchem er wird getabelt werden.
He will be blamed by the man	*by whom he will be blamed.*
Er iſt von demjenigen getabelt worden,	von welchem er getabelt worden iſt.
	or, von welchem er iſt getabelt worden.
He has been blamed by the man	*by whom he has been blamed.*
Er wird von demjenigen getabelt worden ſein,	von welchem er getabelt worden ſein wird.
	or, and better, von welchem er wird getabelt worden ſein.
He will have been blamed by the man.	*by whom he will have been blamed.*

85. A conditional sentence introduced by a subordinating conjunction may also be expressed by
omitting the conjunction and using the order for
questions and commands.

E.g. Wenn er nicht will,

If he will not,

may be expressed by will er nicht.

86. So also after the conjunction als.

E.g. Als wenn er verrückt wäre,

As if he were mad,

may be expressed by als wäre er verrückt.

87. Compounds of wenn and ob with auch, gleich,
schon, zwar, wohl, all meaning "although," may be
divided by one or two words.

E.g. Wenn er es gleich gethan hat.

Although he has done it.

Exercise XI. (from various authors).

(1) Once, after the Piper Assize had been held
(abhalten), my grandfather gave me a present.

(2) Were I not so old, I would dance.

(3) It was not yet declared (ausgesprochen) that war
should (solle, subj. pres.) be waged against the French
oppressors.

(4) The violent wrath of the whole nation seemed
to him like a spell-of-fever (Fieberrausch) which would

soon cool-down (verrauchen) when life and property had to be sacrificed.

(5) I have been praised by the man by whom my brother has been blamed.

(6) He would have been blamed by the man by whom I had been praised.

(7) You ought to have told me.

(8) There was once a beautiful woman, but she was proud and haughty and could not bear to-be (that she should be) surpassed by any one in (an) beauty.

(9) When the fire was just about to be lighted, six swans came flying (gezogen) through the air.

(10) If you love me, keep my commandments.

Write in another possible order :—

(1) Gienge das Ei verloren, so würbe ein großes Unglück daraus entstehen.

Should the egg be lost, a great misfortune would be the result.

(2) Als ob ich ben Kerl getabelt hätte.

As if I had blamed the fellow.

Write in correct order :—

(3) So er trug auch immer einen talarähnlichen Schlafrock und auf bem Haupt eine faltige schwarze Sammtmütze, so baß er hätte eine mittlere Person barstellen können zwischen Alcinous und Laertes.

*Then too he always wore a kind of dressing
gown reaching to the ankles, and a slouching
black velvet cap on his head, so that he might
have represented a personage half way between
Alcinous and Laertes.*

(4) Da der Fall eines der ersten Anführer die jungen
Soldaten erschrecken können hätte, so wurde der
Leichnam mit einem weißen Tuche bedeckt.

*As the fall of one of the chief leaders might
have scared the young soldiers, the corpse was
covered with a white cloth.*

(5) Der Tag herankam, an welchem sollte das Urtheil
werden vollzogen.

*The day approached on which the sentence was
to be carried out.*

Rules. *Group* XII.

88. In subordinate sentences, if the introductory
conjunction **daß** is omitted, the sentence preserves
the **assertive** or categorical **order.**

E.g. Der Hund meinte, **daß** ein paar Knochen ihm
auch gut **thäten.**—Grimm.

*The dog thought that a few bones might do him good
too,*

may be expressed thus:—

Der Hund meinte, ein paar Knochen **thäten** ihm auch
gut.

89. In dependent sentences the finite parts of haben and sein in compound tenses are frequently omitted, so that the past participle stands at the end of a dependent sentence.

E.g. Und rette mich, die du vom Tod errettet,
　　　 Auch von dem Leben hier, dem zweiten Tode.
GOETHE.

And rescue me, whom thou didst save from death,
From this life also, the second death.

Instead of :—

　　　 Die du vom Tod errettet hast.

90. The omission of the auxiliary is frequently only a postponement, the auxiliary being expressed with the last of a series of past participles.

E.g. Wenn du den göttergleichen Agamemnon,
　　　 Der dir sein Liebstes zum Altare brachte,
　　　 Von Troja's umgewandten Mauern rühmlich
　　　 Nach seinem Vaterland zurückbegleitet,
　　　 Die Gattin ihm, Elektren und den Sohn
　　　 Die schönen Schätze, wohl erhalten hast,
　　　 So gieb auch mich den Meinen endlich wieder.
GOETHE.

If thou hast brought back to his fatherland in triumph from Troy's ruins the godlike Agamemnon, who offered his dearest child in sacrifice to thee; if thou hast preserved to him those fair treasures, his wife, his daughter, and his son, then do thou at last restore me too to my people.

The haſt which is **expressed** after erhalten is **understood** with jurückbegleitet.

91. The conjunction und has sometimes a strange influence on the **order** of the following sentence. It **reinstates**, as it were, the **assertive** order.

E.g. Wenn ſie heim kommen und finden dich, ſo ermorden ſie dich.—GRIMM.

When they come home and find you, they will murder you.

Instead of wenn ſie heim kommen und dich finden, an order which, however, is perfectly correct.

92. Some conjunctions have two uses, demonstrative and relative. Such are da, ſo, indem, indeß. .Accordingly we find the copula or copula-containing verb-form sometimes immediately following these conjunctions, and sometimes at the end of the sentence introduced by them.

> *E.g.* Da hat er es gethan.
> *Then he did it.*
>
> Da er es gethan hat.
> *Since he has done it.*
>
> So weit geht meine Freundſchaft.
> *So far does my friendship go.*
>
> So weit meine Freundſchaft geht.
> *As far as my friendship goes.*

E

93. The following are a few among many instances
in which difference of meaning depends entirely upon
difference of order :—

Selbst ich.

Even I.

Ich selbst.

I myself.

Da es regnet.

As it rains.

Da regnet es.

Then it rains.

Indeß gehe ich spazieren.

Meanwhile I go for a walk.

Indeß ich spazieren gehe.

While I go for a walk.

Er fand mühsam den Weg.

He found the way with diffi-
culty.

Er fand den Weg mühsam.

He found the road weari-
some.

Exercise XII.

Translate into German :—

(1) The cock called out to his comrades (that)
there must (subj.) be a house not far off.

(2) She thought she had never seen so great
splendour.

(3) The wolf thought (that) that had (subj.) not
been spoken in earnest.

(4) The witch carried a basket on her back as if
she wished to collect charitable gifts.

(5) He ought to have remembered the warning of
his godfather.

Write in correct order :—

Ein Löwe würdigte einen drolligten Hasen seiner nähern Bekanntschaft. „Aber ist es denn wahr," einst der Hase fragte ihn, „daß ein elender krähender Hahn kann verjagen euch Löwen so leicht ? " „Allerdings es ist wahr," antwortete der Löwe ; „ und es ist eine allgemeine An= merkung, daß wir große Thiere durchgängig haben eine gewisse kleine Schwachheit an uns. So zum Exempel du wirst haben gehört von dem Elephanten daß das Grunzen eines Schweines erweckt ihm Schauder und Entsetzen." „Wahrhaftig ? " unterbrach ihn der Hase. „ Ja, nun ich begreife auch warum wir Hasen fürchten uns so entsetzlich vor den Hunden."—LESSING (altered).

A lion once honoured a merry hare with his friendship. " But is it then true," the hare once asked him, " that a miserable crowing cock can drive you lions away so easily ? " "Certainly it is true," answered the lion ; " indeed it is a common observation that we big animals regularly have some little frailty of our own. For example, you will have heard of the elephant that the grunting of a pig excites in him fear and trembling." " Really ? " interposed the hare. " To be sure, now I understand too why we hares are so terribly frightened of dogs."

SUPPLEMENTARY RULES.

It is no longer regarded as a mark of excellence in German composition to write page-long sentences. Shorter sentences are, as in French and English, preferred.

Greater clearness is aimed at.

One result of this is that in some cases participles, infinitives, and separable particles, are placed earlier in the complex sentence than the strict rules of order would require. It would be wrong now to write :—

Ich habe das Haus, welches ihre Mutter verkauft hat, gesehen.

I have seen the house which your mother has sold.

We must write :—

Ich habe das Haus **gesehen,** welches Ihre Mutter verkauft hat.

It would also be wrong to write :—

Man kann nicht eine genaue Definition von dem, was als ein Thier zu betrachten ist, geben.

We cannot give an exact definition of what is to be regarded as an animal.

We must write :—

Man kann nicht eine genaue Definition von dem geben, was als ein Thier zu betrachten ist.

An objection seems to be felt to the presence of the two verbal forms, each completing its own sentence, in close proximity.

It is to be noticed that we might perfectly well say :—

Man kann nicht von dem, was als ein Thier zu betrachten ist, eine genaue Definition geben.

That is to say, when the infinitive or participle is supported by part of the principal sentence immediately preceding it, this group may well stand after the adjective subordinate sentence.

Notice the order in the following sentence :—

Sie wird einige Tage in der Stadt bei einer recht= schaffenen Frau zubringen, die sich nach der Aussage der Aerzte ihrem Ende naht.—GOETHE.

She will spend a few days in the town with an honest woman, who, the doctors say, is approaching her end.

These remarks may be taken as supplementary especially to § 58; for it is the adjective sentence which is thus generally postponed until after the completion of the principal sentence.

A very nice discrimination is frequently required in order to pick out the most suitable place in a complex sentence for the insertion of the participle or infinitive, or separable particle of the principal sentence.

Looking at this sentence :—

Es sprechen keine Worte die Zartheit, die in seinem ganzen Wesen und Ausdruck war, aus,

we find that the best position for aus is after Zartheit, *i.e.* at the close of the principal sentence, and before the commencement of the subordinate adjective sentence.

Es sprechen keine Worte die Zartheit aus, die in seinem ganzen Wesen und Ausdruck war.—GOETHE.

No words can express the tenderness which informed his whole being and expression.

Examine this sentence :—

Es macht mir großes Vergnügen, Ihnen einen kleinen Gegendienst für die mehrfache Bemühung, die Sie schon für mich gehabt haben, erweisen zu können.

We find the collocation gehabt haben, erweisen zu können clumsy; we look for a place for erweisen zu können, and find it after Gegendienst.

Es macht mir großes Vergnügen, Ihnen einen kleinen Gegendienst **erweisen zu können** für die mehrfache Bemühung, die Sie schon für mich gehabt haben.

It gives me much pleasure to be able to make you some small compensation for the frequent trouble you have had on my behalf.

By the strict rules of order for complex sentences these forms of the predicate—past participle, infinitive, separable particle—should stand in assertive sentences at the extreme end of the complex sentence ; but in order to insure greater clearness they are frequently placed at the end of the principal sentence, especially before adjective sentences.

E.g. Ich habe ein Haus gesehen, welches sehr schön ist.

Ich will Ihnen etwas geben, was sehr gut ist.

Es sprechen keine Worte die Zartheit aus, die in seinem ganzen Wesen und Ausdruck war.—GOETHE.

So also in subordinate sentences which have other sentences subordinate to them, and act the part, to a certain extent, of principal sentences.

Ich gestehe dir gern, daß diejenigen die glücklichsten sind, die gleich den Kindern in den Tag hinein leben.

GOETHE.

I gladly confess to you that those are the happiest who, like children, take no thought for the morrow.

It will be noticed that the subordinate sentence daß diejenigen die glücklichsten sind, is finished before the adjective sentence die gleich den Kindern in den Tag hinein leben is commenced.

And generally it may be said that the present tendency of the German language is to avoid much interweaving of complex sentences, to use as far as possible a succession of short principal sentences, as in French and English, and if complex sentences are necessary, to keep as distinct and separate as possible principal and subordinate sentences.

SUPPLEMENTARY EXERCISES.

(1) Write in correct order:—

Als Hercules ward aufgenommen in den Himmel, er machte seinen Gruß der Juno zuerst unter allen Göttern. Der ganze Himmel und Juno erstaunte(n) darüber. „Deiner Feindin," man zurief ihm, „begegnest du so vorzüglich?" „Ja, ihr selbst," erwiderte Hercules. „Nur ihre Verfolgungen sind es, die (haben) gegeben mir Gelegenheit zu den Thaten, womit ich habe verdient den Himmel." Der Olymp billigte die Antwort des neuen Gottes und Juno ward versöhnt.—Lessing (altered).

When Hercules was taken up into heaven, he greeted Juno first among all the gods. All heaven was astonished, Juno with the rest. "Dost thou bestow such preference on thine enemy?" they cried. "Yes," answered Hercules, "on mine enemy herself. It is her persecutions alone which have given me occasion for those deeds by which I have won a place in heaven." All Olympus approved of the answer of the new god, and Juno was appeased.

(2) Write in correct order:—

Als Jupiter feierte das Fest seiner Vermählung und alle Thiere brachten ihm Geschenke, Juno vermißte das

Schaf. „Wo bleibt das Schaf?" fragte die Göttin.
„Warum versäumt das fromme Schaf zu bringen uns sein
wohlmeinendes Geschenk?" Und der Hund nahm auf das
Wort und sprach: „Zürne nicht, Göttin. Ich habe noch
heute gesehen das Schaf: es war sehr betrübt und jam=
merte laut." „Und warum jammerte das Schaf?" fragte
die schon gerührte Göttin. „Ich ärmste!" so sprach es,
„ich habe jetzt weder Wolle, noch Milch: was werde ich
schenken dem Jupiter? Soll ich, ich allein scheinen leer
vor ihm? Lieber ich will hingehen, und bitten den
Hirten, daß er opfere mich ihm!" Indem drang mit
des Hirten Gebet der Rauch des geopferten Schafes, dem
Jupiter ein süßer Geruch durch die Wolken. Und jetzt
Juno hätte geweint die erste Thräne wenn Thränen
benetzten ein unsterbliches Auge.—LESSING (altered).

*When Jupiter was celebrating the festival of his
marriage, and all the animals were bringing him
presents, Juno missed the sheep. " Where is the sheep ?"
asked the goddess. " Why does the pious sheep neglect
to bring us its affectionate gift ?" And the dog took up
the word and said, " Be not angry, goddess ! This very
day I saw the sheep; it was much troubled, and
lamented aloud." " And why did the sheep lament ?"
asked the goddess, already touched. " ' Ah, wretched
me !' it said, ' I have now neither wool nor milk;
what shall I present to Jupiter ? Shall I, I alone,
appear empty before him ? Rather I will go and beg
the shepherd to offer me in sacrifice to him.'" Meanwhile the smoke of the sacrifice, to Jupiter a sweet-
smelling savour, penetrated through the clouds with the*

prayer of the shepherd. And now Juno would have wept her first tear, if ever tears moistened the eye of an immortal.

(3) Write in correct order :—

Herr Oscar Wilde traf ein hier geſtern Abend. Die Vertreter der Morgenblätter ſogleich erſtiegen den Dampfer im untern Hafen, und veröffentlichen dieſen Morgen genaue Beſchreibungen über ſeine perſönliche Erſcheinung, Kleidung, und Unterhaltungsweiſe. Herr Wilde behauptete zu ſein enttäuſcht mit dem atlantiſchen Meere.

*Mr. Oscar Wilde arrived last evening. The reporters of the morning papers boarded the steamer in the lower bay, and publish this morning minute descriptions of his personal appearance, dress, and style of conversation. Mr. Wilde expressed himself as " disappointed " with the Atlantic.—*DAILY NEWS.

(4) Write in correct order :—

Ich habe aus den beſten Quellen, daß die Söhne des öſtreichiſchen Kaiſers zankten ſich furchtbar eines Tages. Als nun eben der eine Sohn ſagte dem andern, „ Du biſt der größte Eſel in Wien," der Vater erſchien im Thürgang und ſagte, „ Ihr vergeßt, junge Herren, daß ich bin anweſend." So gut war der Spaß, daß aller Zwieſpalt löſte ſich auf in lebhaftes Lachen ; und Vater und Söhne brachten den Abend mit einander recht luſtig zu.

I have heard on good authority that the sons of the Emperor of Austria were quarrelling desperately one day, when just as one said to the other, " You are the greatest ass in Vienna," the father appeared in the doorway and said gravely, " You forget, young gentlemen, that I am present." So good was the joke, that all differences were merged in a hearty laugh, and parent and children spent the evening together right merrily.

EXAMINER.

(5) Write in correct order:—

Muggleton war am Spiele zuerst, und groß war die Spannung, als Mr. Dumkins und Mr. Podder, zwei der ausgezeichnetsten Clubmitglieder, begaben sich, die Ball= hölzer in der Hand, nach ihren Wickets. Mr. Luffey, Dingley Dells höchste Zier, war gewählt, zu schleudern den Ball gegen des furchtbaren Dumkins Wicket, und Mr. Struggles war ausersehen zu erweisen denselben Dienst dem bis auf diesen Tag unüberwundenen Podder. An verschiedenen Plätzen Spieler waren aufgestellt als Aufpasser, und setzten sich in gehörige Positur, indem sie bückten sich ein wenig, und hemmten die Hände auf die Kniee. Alle regelrechten Cricketspieler machen es so; denn nimmt man als ausgemacht an, daß es sei unmöglich, aufzupassen gehörig in einer andern Stellung.

SEYBT'S TRANSLATION OF THE PICKWICK PAPERS (altered).

All Muggleton had the first innings, and the interest became intense when Mr. Dumkins and Mr. Podder,

two of the most renowned members of that most dis-
tinguished club, walked, bat in hand, to their respective
wickets. Mr. Luffey, the highest ornament of Dingley
Dell, was pitched to bowl against the redoubtable Dum-
kins, and Mr. Struggles was selected to do the same kind
office for the hitherto unconquered Podder. Several
players were stationed to " look out " in different parts
of the field, and each fixed himself into the proper
attitude by placing one hand on each knee. All
the regular players do this sort of thing, indeed it's
generally supposed that it is quite impossible to look out
properly in any other position.

(6) Write in correct order:—

Wenn ein Vater erzählt seinem Kinde, daß dieser oder
jener Mann verschmachte vor Armuth, und das Kind
hingeht und dem armen Mann seines Vaters Geldbörse
zuträgt, so diese Handlung ist naiv: denn die gesunde
Natur handelte aus dem Kinde, und in einer Welt, wo
die gesunde Natur herrschte, es würde gehabt haben voll=
kommen Recht, zu verfahren so. Es sieht bloß auf das
Bedürfniß und auf das nächste Mittel, zu befriedigen es;
eine solche Ausdehnung des Eigenthumsrechtes, wobei
ein Theil der Menschen kann gehen zu Grunde, ist nicht
gegründet in der bloßen Natur. Die Handlung des
Kindes ist also eine Beschämung der wirklichen Welt, und
das unser Herz gesteht auch durch das Wohlgefallen,
welches es empfindet über jene Handlung.

SCHILLER (altered).

When a father tells his child that such and such a man is languishing in poverty, and the child goes and carries his father's purse to the poor man, this action is naïve ; for the child's uncontaminated nature prompted the deed, and in a world in which nature uncontaminated bore sway, the child would have been perfectly right in acting thus. The child looks only at the need, and at the nearest means of satisfying the need. An extension of the right of property, by which one part of mankind may perish, has no foundation in mere nature. The action of the child thus puts the actual world to shame, and this our heart, too, confesses by the pleasurable emotion which it experiences in the contemplation of the deed.

(7) Write in correct order :—

Es trug einmal ein Philosoph des Alterthums etwas unter seinem Mantel. Als nun ein Bekannter desselben verlangte von ihm, daß er möge laſſen ihn wiſſen, was er verſtecke ſo ſorgfältig, er antwortete, „ Ich verſtecke es eben deßhalb, damit ihr wiſſet nicht es.‟

*An ancient philosopher was carrying something hidden under his cloak. A certain acquaintance desiring him to let him know what it was he covered so carefully, " I cover it," says he, " on purpose that you should not know."—*Spectator.

(8) Write in correct order :—

„ Erinnerſt du dich nicht, mein Kind,‟ ſie ſagte, „ daß der Taubenſchlag einfiel denſelben Nachmittag, als unſere gedankenloſe Magd ſchüttete das Salz über den

Tiſch?" „Ja, mein Liebſtes," er ſagte, „und die folgende Poſt uns Nachricht brachte von der Schlacht bei Almanza."

"Do you not remember, child," says she, "that the pigeon-house fell the very afternoon that our careless wench spilt the salt upon the table?" "Yes," says he, "my dear, and the next post brought us an account of the battle of Almanza."—SPECTATOR.

(9) Write in correct order :—

Als wir ſtanden vor Buſby's Grabmal, der Ritter äußerte ſich auf dieſelbe Weiſe nochmals. „Dr. Buſby, ein großer Mann! Er prügelte meinen Großvater; ein ſehr großer Mann! Ich wäre gegangen zu ihm ſelbſt in die Schule, wenn ich wäre nicht geweſen ein Dumm= kopf; ein ſehr großer Mann!"

As we stood before Busby's tomb the knight uttered himself again after the same manner. "Dr. Busby, a great man! He whipped my grandfather; a very great man! I should have gone to him myself if I had not been a blockhead; a very great man!

SPECTATOR.

(10) Write in correct order :—

Da Sir Roger iſt der ganzen Gemeinde Gutsherr ſo hält er ſie während des Gottesdienſtes in ſehr guter Ordnung, und läßt Niemand, außer ſich einſchlafen. Denn, wenn er während der Predigt iſt zufällig eingenickt und dann wieder kommt zu ſich, ſo ſteht er auf und ſchaut um ſich. Falls er ſieht Jemand anders nicken,

er weckt ihn entweder selber auf oder schickt seinen Diener
zu ihm. Noch einige andere Sonderbarkeiten des Ritters
kommen zum Vorschein bei solchen Gelegenheiten. So er
pflegt zuweilen zu ausdehnen einen Vers aus den Psalmen
eine halbe Minute nach allen übrigen Mitsängern in
der Gemeinde. Ein anderes Mal, wenn der Inhalt
seines Gebetes besonders gefällt ihm, er sagt nach dem
nämlichen Gebete Amen drei= oder viermal; und manch=
mal er aufsteht, wenn alle Uebrigen niederknien, um zu
zählen die Gemeinde, oder um zu sehen, ob etwa Einer
von seinen Pächtern fehlt.

*As Sir Roger is landlord to the whole congregation,
he keeps them in very good order, and will suffer nobody to sleep in it besides himself; for if by chance he
has been surprised into a short nap at sermon, upon
recovering out of it he stands up and looks about him,
and if he sees anybody else nodding, either wakes them
himself or sends his servants to them. Several other of
the old knight's peculiarities break out upon these occa-
sions: sometimes he will be lengthening out a verse in
the singing psalms half a minute after the rest of the
congregation have done with it; sometimes when he is
pleased with the matter of his devotion, he pronounces*
Amen *three or four times to the same prayer; and
sometimes stands up, when everybody else is upon their
knees, to count the congregation, or see if any of his
tenants are missing.*—SPECTATOR.

(11) Write in correct order:—

Kurz gesagt! ich fand nach dem Berichte meines
Freundes, daß er besaß eine ausgezeichnete Gesundheit,

aber sonst nichts ; und daß, wenn es wäre die einzige Aufgabe des Menschen bloß zu leben, kein ausgebildeterer junger Mann wäre zu finden im ganzen Lande.

To be brief, I found by my friend's account of him that he had got a great stock of health, but nothing else ; and that if it were a man's business only to live, there would not be a more accomplished young fellow in the whole country.—SPECTATOR.

(12) Write in correct order :—

Meine erste Wohnung ich mußte verlassen wegen einer zudringlichen Hauswirthin, die bestand darauf zu fragen mich jeden Morgen, wie ich hätte geschlafen.

I was obliged to quit my first lodgings by reason of an officious landlady, that would be asking me every morning how I slept.—SPECTATOR.

VOCABULARY.

N.B.—Nouns are given with the article in the nominative singular, and are repeated in the genitive singular and nominative plural. The personal pronouns are declined.

Verbs are given in the infinitive present, and are repeated in the past tense and past participle if there is any irregularity in the conjugation. The present indicative is also given, if it is irregular, in brackets before the past tense.

F 2

A.

A, an, ein, eine, ein, a.

be About, followed by infinitive, follen (foll), follte, gefollt or follen, v.i., h.

be Absent, fehlen, v.r., h., dat.

Acquire, erwerben, erwarb, erworben, v.i., h., acc.

Action, die Handlung, —, —en, n.

Actor, der Schauspieler, —s, —, n.

be Afraid, sich fürchten, v.r. (be afraid) of, vor, dat.

After, nach, prep., dat. ; nachdem, c.s.

Again, wieder, adv.

Against, gegen, wider, prep., acc.

Ah, ach, int.

Air, die Luft, —, Lüfte, n.

Al Hafi, Al Hafi, —s, n.

All, all, a. ; all at once, auf einmal.

Almost, beinahe, fast, adv.

Alone, allein, a. ; predicative only.

Always, immer, adv.

Among, unter, prep., acc., and dat.

And, und, c.c.

Angel, der Engel, —s, —, n.

Animal, das Thier, —es, —e, n.

Answer, die Antwort, —, —en, n. ; antworten, erwiedern, versetzen v.r., h., dat.

Ant, die Ameise, —, —n, n.

Any one, Jemand, p.

Appear, erscheinen, erschien, erschienen, v.i., s.

Appease (of hunger or thirst) stillen, v.r., h., acc.

Arrive, ankommen, kam an, angekommen, v.i., s.

As, wie, als, c.s. ; as = since, da, c.s. ; as if, als ob, c.s. ; as long as, so lange, c.s.

Ashes, die Asche, —. The German singular is equivalent to the English plural.

Ask, fragen, fragte or frug, gefragt, v.i., h., acc.

Astonishment, das Erstaunen, —s, n.

At, an, in, bei, zu, prep., dat. ; at the end, am Ende ; at last endlich ; at Paris, zu Paris or in Paris.

Aunt, die Tante, —, —n, n.

Author, der Schriftsteller, —s, —, n.

Awaken, wachen, aufwachen, v.r., h. ; wecken, aufwecken, v.r., h., acc.

B.

Back, zurück, adv. ; der Rücken, —s, —, n.

Basket, der Korb, —es, Körbe, n.

Bath-tub, die Wanne, —, —n, n.

Be, sein (bin), war, gewesen, v.i., s.

Bear = endure, suffer, leiden, litt, gelitten, v.i., h., acc.

Beast, das Thier, —es, —e, n.

Beat, schlagen, schlug, geschlagen, v.i., h., acc.

Beautiful, schön, a.

Beauty, die Schönheit, —, —en, n.

Because, da, weil, c.s.

Become, werden, ward or wurde, geworden, v.i., s.

Bed, das Bett, —es, —en, n.

Before, vor, prep., acc. and dat. ; bevor, ehe, c.s.

Beggar, der Bettler, —s, —, n.

Believe, glauben, meinen, v.r., h., acc.

Bench, die Bank, —, Bänke, n.

Berlin, (das) Berlin, —s, n.

Big, groß, a.

Blame, tadeln, v.r., h., acc.

Boat, das Schiff, —es, —e ; das Boot, —es, —e, or Böte, n.

Book, das Buch, —es, Bücher, n.

Box, die Schachtel, —, —n ; die Kiste, —, —n, n.

Boy, der Knabe, —n, —n, n.

Bremen, (das) Bremen, —s, n.

Bring, bringen, brachte, gebracht, v.i., h., acc.

Brother, der Bruder, —s, Brüder, n.

Bush, der Strauch, —es, Sträuche, and Sträucher, n.

But, aber, ſonbern, c.c., außer, prep. dat. ; nothing but, nichts als.

By, an, bei ; von, prep. dat. ; burch, prep. acc.

C.

Call, rufen, rief, gerufen, v.i., h., acc. ; call out to, zurufen, rief zu, zugerufen, v.i., h., dat.

be Called, named, heißen, hieß, geheißen, v.i., h.

Can, können (kann), konnte, gekonnt or können, v.i., h.

Carry, tragen, trug, getragen, v.i., h., acc.

(Catch sight of, erbliden, v.r., h., acc.)

Cause, laſſen, ließ, gelaſſen or laſſen, v.i., h., acc.

Certainly, gewiß, ohne Zweifel, adv.

Character, ber Character, —s, —e ; ber Typus, — ; Typen, n.

Charitable gifts, milbe Gaben.

Child, bas Kinb, —es, —er, n.

Christian, ber Chriſt, —en, —en, n. ; chriſtlich, a.

Cinderella, (bie) Aſchenbröbel, —, n.

Circumstance, ber Umſtanb, —es, Umſtäube.

Clean, ſauber, a.

Clever, klug, a.

Cloth, bas Tuch, —es, Tücher, n. ; little cloth, bas Tüchlein, —s, —, n.

Cock, ber Hahn, —es, Hähne, n.

Collect, ſammeln, v.r., h., acc.

Come, kommen, kam, gekommen, v.i., s.

Commandment, bas Gebot, —es, —e, n.

Company, bie Geſellſchaft, —, —en.

Complete, völlig, vollſtänbig, a.

Comrade, ber Geſell(e), —en, —en, n.

Conduct, bringen, brachte, gebracht, v.i., h., acc.

Conformable, gemäß, a.

Constantinople, (bas) Conſtantinopel, —s, n.

Contented, zufrieben, a.

Count, ber Graf, —en, —en, n.

Courtyard, ber Hof, —es, Höfe, n.

Cover, beden, bebeden, v.r., h., acc. ; covered, bebedt, a.

Coverlet, die Bettdecke, —, —n, n.

Cradle, die Wiege, —, —n, n.

Crisis, der Entscheidungspunkt, —es, Entscheidungspünkte ; die Krisis, —, Krisen, n.

Crusade, der Kreuzzug, —es, Kreuzzüge, n.

Cry, schreien, schrie, geschrieen, v.i., h.

Cudgel, der Knüppel, —s, —, n.

Cut, schneiden, schnitt, geschnitten, v.i., h., acc.

D.

Dance, tanzen, v.r., h.

Daughter, die Tochter, —, Töchter, n.

Day, der Tag, —es, —e, n.

Dear, lieb, a.

Death, der Tod, —es, Todesfälle, n.

Deathbed, das Sterbebett, —es, —en, n.

Declare, erklären, v.r., h., acc., or express by doch, I declare I have = habe ich doch.

Deserted, einsam, a.

Die, sterben, starb, gestorben, v.i., s.

Diplomatist, der Diplomat, —en, —en, n.

Dirty, schmutzig, a.

Disguise, die Verkleidung, —, —en, n. ; see Guise.

Disposition, die Gesinnung, —, —en, n.

Do, thun, that, gethan, v.i., h., acc. ; machen, v.r., h., acc.

Doctor, der Arzt, —es, Aerzte, n.

Dog, der Hund, —es, —e, n.

Down, nieder, adv.

Dramatic, dramatisch, a.

Drink, trinken, trank, getrunken, v.i., h., acc.

During, während, prep., genitive.

Dwarf, der Zwerg, —es, —e, n.

E.

Earnest, ernsthaft, a. ; in earnest, mit Ernst.

Easy, leicht, a.

Eat, effen, aß, gegeffen, v.i., h., acc.

Embroider, ſticken, v.r., h., acc.

End, das Ende, —s, —n, n.

Enemy, der Feind, —es, —e, n.

Englishman, der Engländer, —s, —, n.

Envious, neidiſch, a.

European, europäiſch, a. ; der Europäer, —s, —, n.

Even, ſelbſt, auch, adv.

Evening, der Abend, —s, —e, n.

Every one, ein Jeder, ein Jeglicher, p.

Excellent, vortreſſlich, a.

Excuse, entſchulbigen, v.r., h., acc., to be excused = zu ent=
ſchulbigen.

Experience, of feeling, empfinden, empfand, empfunden; of
knowledge, erfahren, erfuhr, erfahren, v.i., h., acc.

Experience, die Erfahrung, —, —en, n.

F.

Failing, der Fehler, —s, — ; das Fehlen, —s, n.

Faith, der Glaube(n), —ns, n.

Fall, fallen, fiel, gefallen, v.i., s.

Far, weit, a. and adv. ; as far as, ſo weit, c.s.

Father, der Vater, —s, Väter, n.

Faust, der Fauſt, n.

Feather, die Feder, —, —n, n.

Fire, das Feuer, —s, —, n.

First, erſt, a.

Following, folgend, nächſt, a.

For, für, prep., acc. : denn, c.c.

Foreigner, der Fremde, —n, —n ; ein Fremder, plural Fremde.

Form, bilden, v.r., h., acc.

Fox, der Fuchs, —es, Füchſe, n.

Friend, der Freund, —es, —e, n.

From, aus, von, prep., dat.

Furious, raſend, a.

G.

Ganges, ber Ganges, —, n.

Gaping, ben Mund aufreißend, a.

Get = cause, get done, thun lassen ; see Cause.

Giant, ber Riese, —n, —n, n.

Give, geben, gab, gegeben, v.i., h., dat. and acc.

Go, gehen, ging, gegangen, v.i., s.

Go away, weggehen, ging weg, weg gegangen, v.i., s.

Godfather, ber Gevatter, —s, — ; ber Pathe, —n, —n, n.

Gold, bas Gold, —es, n.

Golden, golben, a.

Goldsmith, ber Goldschmieb, —es, —e, n.

Gracious, gnäbig, a.

Grandfather, ber Großvater, —s, Großväter, n.

Grandmother, bie Großmutter, —, Großmütter, n.

Grave, bas Grab, —es, Gräber, n.

Great, groß, a.

Guise, bie Gestalt, —, —en, n.

H.

Habit, bie Gewohnheit, —, —en, n.

Hair, bas Haar, —es, —e, n.

Hardly, kaum, adv.

Haughty, übermüthig, a.

Have, haben, hatte, gehabt, v.i., h., acc.

He, er, seiner, ihm, ihn, p.

Heart, bas Herz, —ens, —en, n.

Hearth, ber Herb, —es, —e, n.

Her, ihr, ihre, ihr, a.

Here, hier, adv. ; from here, von hinnen, adv.

High, hoch, a.   In oblique cases ch changed to h.

Himself, herself, itself, themselves, sich.

His, sein, seine, sein, a.

Hold, halten, hielt, gehalten, v.i., h., acc.

Hole, bie Grube, —, —n, n.

Hollow, hohl, a.
Honest, ehrlich, rechtschaffen, redlich, a.
Hood, die Kappe, —, —n ; little hood, das Käppchen, —s, —, n.
Horse, das Pferd, —es, —e, n.
House, das Haus, —es, Häuser, n.
How ? wie? adv.
However, aber, indessen, jedoch, c.c.
Hunger, der Hunger, —s, n.
Huntsman, der Jäger, —s, —, n.
Hypocrite, der Heuchler, —s, —, n.

I.

I, ich, meiner, mir, mich, p.
Idea, die Idee, —, —n, n.
Idle, faul, n.
If, wenn, c.s.
Impatient, ungeduldig, a.
Important, bedeutend, a.
In, in, prep. ; dat., see Into.
Industriously, fleißig, adv.
Inherit, erben, ererben, v.r., h., acc. ; erhalten, erhielt, erhalten,
    v.i., h., acc.
Interesting, unterhaltend, a.
Into, in, prep., acc. ; see In.
Islam, der Islam, —s, n.
It, es, dessen or davon, ihm, es, p.
Ivory, das Elfenbein, —s, n.

J.

John, (der) Johann, —s, n.
Just, eben, adv.

K.

Keep, halten, hielt, gehalten, v.i., h., acc.
Kind, gütig, a.
King, der König, —es, —e, n.

Know, of facts (Lat., scire, Fr., savoir), miſſen, mußte, gewußt, v.i., h., acc. ; of places and persons (Lat., novisse, Fr., connaître), fennen, fannte, gefannt, v.i., h., acc.

L.

Language, bie Sprache, —, —n, n.

Last, leßt, a. ; see At last.

Lay, legen, v.r., h., acc.

Lead, führen, v.r., h., acc.

Leafless, laublos, blätterlos, a.

Learn, lernen, v.r., h., acc.

Leather, bas Leber, —8, n.

Leave, laſſen, ließ, gelaſſen, v.i., h., acc.

Leave off, aufhören, hörte auf, aufgehört, v.r., h., acc.

Left, übrig, a.; be left, übrig bleiben.

Let = allow or cause, laſſen, ließ, gelaſſen, v.i., h., acc.

Letter, ber Brief, —es, —e, n.

Lie, liegen, lag, gelegen, v.i., h. and s.

Life, bas Leben, —8 ; life and property, Gut unb Blut.

Light = kindle, anzünben, zünbete an, angezünbet, v.r., h., acc.

Like, gleich, a. and adv., dat. ; wie, c.s.

Little, flein, a. ; or express by diminutive in -chen or -lein.

Little Red Riding Hood, bas Rothfäppchen, —8, n.

Live, leben, wohnen, v.r., h.

Lofty, erhaben, a.

London, (bas) Lonbon, —8, n.

Longing (for), bie Sehnſucht (nach).

Look at, anſehen, ſah an, angeſehen, v.i., h., acc.

Lore, bie Lehre, —, —n, n.

Loud, laut, a. ; comparative, lauter.

Love, bie Liebe, —, —n, n. ; lieben, v.r., h., acc.

Low, niebrig, a.

M.

Main thing, bie Hauptſache, —, —n, n.

Make, machen, v.r., h., acc.

Man, der Mann, —es, Männer, or in certain cases Mann or Mannen; der Mensch, —en, —en, n.

Many, viele, a.

Market, der Markt, —es, Märkte, n.

Mask, die Larve, —, —n, n.

May, der Mai, —es, —e and —en, n.

May, dürfen (darf), durfte, gedurft or dürfen, v.i., h. ; können (kann), konnte, gekonnt or können, v.i., h.

Medicine, die Arznei, —, —en, n.

Meet, entgegenkommen, kam entgegen, entgegengekommen, v.i., s., dat.

More, mehr, a. and adv.

Morning, der Morgen, —s, —, n.

Mother, die Mutter, —, Mütter, n.

Mountain, der Berg, —es, —e, n.

Multitude, die Menge, —, —n, n.

Must, müssen (muß), mußte, gemußt or müssen, v.i., h.

N.

Nation, das Volk, —es, Völker, n.

Natural, natürlich, a.

Nature, die Natur, —, n.

Naughty, unartig, a.

Near, bei, prep., dat.

Neighbourhood, die Nähe, —, —n; die Nachbarschaft, —, —en, n.

Never, of past time, nie, niemals ; of future time, nie, nimmer, nimmermehr, adv.

Next, nächst, folgend, a.

Night, die Nacht, —, Nächte, n.

No, kein, keine, kein, a.

Nobility, der Adel, —s, n.

Nobody, no one, Niemand, —s, p.

North wind, der Nordwind, —es, —e, n.

Not, nicht, adv. ; not yet, noch nicht.

Nothing, Nichts, p. ; nothing but, Nichts als.

Now, jetzt, adv. ; nun, c.a.

Nut, die Nuß, —, Nüsse, n.

O.

Oak, bie Eiche, —, —n, n.

Oblige, zwingen, zwang, gezwungen, v.i., h., acc. ; be obliged, müssen (muß), mußte, gemußt, v.i., h.

Of, von, prep., dat. ; or express by genitive ; of = made of, von or aus, prep., dat.

Off = away, davon, adv.

Offend, beleidigen, v.r., h., acc.

Often, oft, häufig, adv. ; as often as, so oft, c.s.

Old, alt, a.

On, auf, prep., acc. and dat. ; on the third day, an bem britten Tag.

Once, einmal, einst, adv.

One, ein, eine, ein ; one = single, einzig, a.

One, man, oblique cases formed from Einer, p.

Only, nur, adv.

Opposite, bas Gegentheil, —s, —e, n.

Oppressor, ber Unterbrücker, —s, —, n.

Over, über, prep., acc. and dat.

Own, eigen, a.

P.

Pair, bas Paar, —es, — e, also unchanged in plural, n.

Parsee, ber Parser, —s, —, n.

Pass = spend, zubringen, brachte zu, zugebracht, v.i., h., acc. ; pass the night, übernachten, v.r., h.

Patient, ber Kranke, —n, —n, n.

Peacefully, ruhig, adv.

Peasant, ber Bauer, —n, —n, sometimes —s, —, n.

Picture, bas Gemälbe, —s, —, n.

Pick up, auflesen, las auf, aufgelesen, v.i., h., acc.

Pious, fromm, a.

Piper Assize, bas Pfeifergericht, —es, —e, n.

Pitiable, armselig, erbärmlich, a.

Pity, bas Mitleib, —s ; bas Mitleiben, — s ; bas Erbarmen, — s, n.

Place, der Ort, —es, —e, and Oerter, n.

Plan, entwerfen, entwarf, entworfen, v.i., h., acc.

Please, gefallen, gefiel, gefallen, v.i., h., dat.

Poor, arm, a.

Praise, loben, v.r., h., acc.

Predilection, die Vorliebe, —, —n, n.

Present, das Geschenk, —es, —e, n.

Present, schenken, v.r., h., dat. and acc.

Property, das Eigenthum, —es, Eigenthümer; die Habe, — ;
　　life and property, Gut und Blut.

Proposal, der Anschlag, —es, Anschläge, n.

Proud of, stolz auf, acc.

Prove, beweisen, bewies, bewiesen, v.i., h., dat. and acc.

Q.

Queen, die Königin, —, Königinnen, n.

R.

Rank, der Stand, —es, Stände ; der Rang, —es, Ränge, r

Reach = arrive at, erreichen, v.r., h., acc.

Really, wirklich, adv.

Red, roth, a.

Religion, die Religion, —, —en, n.

Religious, religiös, a.

Remain, bleiben, blieb, geblieben, v.i., s.

Remember, sich erinnern, erinnerte sich, sich erinnert, v.r., h.,
　　genitive or an, acc.

Reply, antworten, erwiedern, versetzen, v.r., h., dat.

Rest, die Ruhe, —, —n, n.

Return, zurückkommen, kam zurück, zurückgekommen, v.i., ι

Richly garnished, reichbesetzt, a.

Right, recht, richtig, a.

Ring, der Ring, —es, —e, n.

Room, das Zimmer, —s, —, n.

Root, die Wurzel, —, —n, n.

S.

Sacred, heilig, a.

Sacrifice, zum Opfer bringen, brachte zum Opfer, zum Opfer gebracht, v.i., h., acc.

Salutary, heilsam, a.

Save, retten, v.r., h., acc.

Say, sagen, v.r., h., acc. and dat.

Scene, die Scene, —, —n, n.

Schiller, (der) Schiller, —s, n.

See, sehen, sah, gesehen, v.r., h., acc.

Seem, scheinen, schien, geschienen, v.i., h.

Self, selber or selbst, a. ; I myself, ich selber.

Servant, der Diener, —s, — ; das Dienstmädchen, —s, — ; der Knecht, —es, —e ; die Magd, —, Mägde, n.

Set, setzen, stellen, v.r., h., acc. ; set up, aufstellen, stellte auf, aufgestellt, v.r., h., acc.

Seven, sieben, a.

Several, einige, etliche, mehrere, verschiedene, a.

Shall, sollen (soll), sollte, gesollt or sollen, v.i, h.

She, sie, ihrer, ihr, sie, p.

Shoe, der Schuh, —es, —e, n.

Shoemaker, der Schuster, —s, —, n.

Show, zeigen, v.r., h., dat. and acc.

Shudder, schaubern, v.r., h.

Sigh, seufzen, v.r., h.

Sight = catch sight of, erblicken, v.r., h., acc.

Single, einzig, a.

Sink, sinken, sank, gesunken, v.i., s.

Sit, sitzen, saß, gesessen, v.i., h. and s.

Sittah, (die) Sittah, —, n.

Sleeping room, das Schlafgemach, —es, Schlafgemächer ; das Schlafzimmer, —s, —, n.

Smashed, zerschmettert, a.

So, so, also, adv.

Solomon, (der) Salomon, —s, n.

Son, der Sohn, —es, Söhne, n.

Soon, balb, adv.
Speak, sprechen, sprach, gesprochen, v.i., h., acc.
Splendour, der Glanz, —es; die Pracht, —, n.
Spray, der Schaum, —es, Schäume, n.
Spread, of table = cover, decken, v.r., h., acc.
Stepbrother, der Stiefbruder, —s, Stiefbrüder, n.
Stick, der Stock, —es, Stöcke, n.
Still, noch, adv., = quiet, ruhig, still, a.
Stormy, stürmisch, a.
Strange, fremd, sonderbar, a.
Street, die Straße, —, —n, n.
Strength, die Stärke, —, n.
Strong, stark, a.
Study-table, der Stubirtisch, —es, —e, n.
Stupid, dumm, a.
Suit, passen, v.r., h., dat.
Summer, der Sommer, —s, —, n.
Sunrise, der Sonnenaufgang, —es, Sonnenaufgänge, n.
Surpass, übertreffen, übertraf, übertroffen, v.i., h., acc.
Sustain, erhalten, erhielt, erhalten, v.i., h., acc.
Swan, der Schwan, —es, Schwäne, n.
Swim, schwimmen, schwamm, geschwommen, v.i., h. and s.
Switzerland, die Schweiz, —, n.

T.

Table, der Tisch, —es, —e, n.
Tailor, der Schneider, —s, —, n.
Teacher, der Lehrer, —s, —, n.
Tell, sagen, erzählen, v.r., h., dat. and acc.
Than, als, c.s.
That, daß, c.s.; jener, a. and p.
The, der, die, das, a.
Then, da, dann, darauf, c a.
Thereupon, darauf, c.a.
They, sie, ihrer, ihnen, sie, p.

Think, denfen, dachte, gedacht, v.i., h. ; an Einen.
This, dieser, a.
Thou, du, deiner, dir, dich.
Three, drei, a.
Through, durch, prep., acc.
Time, die Zeit, —, —en, n. ; in music der Tact, —es, —e, n.
Tom Thumb (der) Daumesdick, —es, n.
Tree, der Baum, —es, Bäume, n.
True, wahr, a.
Two, zwei, a.

U.

Under, unter, prep., dat. or acc.
Understand, verstehen, verstand, verstanden, v.i., h., acc.
Until, bis. prep., acc. ; bis zu, prep., dat. ; bis, c.s.

V.

Vanity, die Eitelkeit, —, —en, n.
Velvet, der Sammt, —s, n.
Venture, sich wagen, wagte sich, sich gewagt, v.r., h.
Very, sehr, höchst, adv.
Vigorously, kräftig, adv.
Violent, gewaltig, a.

W.

Wage, führen, v.r., h., acc.
Walk, gehen, ging, gegangen, v.i., s.
Walking, das Gehen, —s, n.
be Wanting, fehlen, v.r., h., dat.
War, der Krieg, —es, —e, n.
Warning, die Warnung, —, —en, n.
Way, der Weg, —es, —e, n.
We, wir, unser, uns, uns, p.
Well, gut, wohl, adv.
Well acquainted with, kundig, a. with genitive.
Well known, bekannt, berühmt, a.

G

What ? was? p.

When ? wann? adv.

When of past time, als, nachdem; of future time or when
    equivalent to whenever, wenn, c.s.

Where ? wo? adv.

Where, wo, c.s.

While, während, c.s.

Who ? wer? p.

Who, der, welcher, relative p.

Whole, ganz, a.

Wife, die Frau, —, —en, n.

Window, das Fenster, —s, —, n.

Wish, wollen (will), wollte, gewollt or wollen, v.i., h. ; wünschen,
    v.r., h.

Wit, der Verstand, —es ; der Witz, —es, n.

Witch, die Hexe, —, —n, n.

With, mit, prep., dat.

Without, ohne, prep., acc.

Witty, witzig, a.

Wolf, der Wolf, —es, Wölfe, n.

Woman, die Frau, —, —en, n.

Wood, der Wald, —es, Wälder, n.

Word, das Wort, —es, —e, and Wörter, n.

Work, die Arbeit, —, —en ; das Werk, —es, —e, n. ; arbeiten,
    v.r., h.

World, die Welt, —, —en, n.

Wrath, der Zorn, —es ; die Wuth, —, n.

Write, schreiben, schrieb, geschrieben, v.i., h., acc.

Y.

Yes, ja, adv. or int.

Yet, noch, adv. ; not yet, noch nicht.

You, ihr, euer, euch, euch, or Sie, Ihrer, Ihnen, Sie, p.

Your, euer, euere, euer, or Ihr, Ihre, Ihr, a.

November 1882.

A CLASSIFIED LIST

OF

EDUCATIONAL WORKS

PUBLISHED BY

GEORGE BELL & SONS.

Full Catalogues will be sent post free on application.

BIBLIOTHECA CLASSICA.

A Series of Greek and Latin Authors, with English Notes, edited by eminent Scholars. 8vo.

Æschylus. By F. A. Paley, M.A. 18s.

Cicero's Orations. By G. Long, M.A. 4 vols. 16s., 14s., 16s., 18s.

Demosthenes. By R. Whiston, M.A. 2 vols. 16s. each.

Euripides. By F. A. Paley, M.A. 3 vols. 16s. each.

Homer. By F. A. Paley, M.A. Vol. I. 12s.; Vol. II. 14s.

Herodotus. By Rev. J. W. Blakesley, B.D. 2 vols. 32s.

Hesiod. By F. A. Paley, M.A. 10s. 6d.

Horace. By Rev. A. J. Macleane, M.A. 18s.

Juvenal and Persius. By Rev. A. J. Macleane, M.A. 12s.

Plato. By W. H. Thompson, D.D. 2 vols. 7s. 6d. each.

Sophocles. Vol. I. By Rev. F. H. Blaydes, M.A. 18s.

———— Vol. II. Philoctetes. Electra. Ajax and Trachiniæ. By F. A. Paley, M.A. 12s.

Tacitus: The Annals. By the Rev. P. Frost. 15s.

Terence. By E. St. J. Parry, M.A. 18s.

Virgil. By J. Conington, M.A. 3 vols. 14s. each.

An Atlas of Classical Geography; Twenty-four Maps. By W. Hughes and George Long, M.A. New edition, with coloured outlines. Imperial 8vo. 12s. 6d.

Uniform with above.

A Complete Latin Grammar. By J. W. Donaldson, D.D. 3rd Edition. 14s.

GRAMMAR-SCHOOL CLASSICS.

A Series of Greek and Latin Authors, with English Notes. Fcap. 8vo.

Cæsar: De Bello Gallico. By George Long, M.A. 5s. 6d.

———— Books I.–III. For Junior Classes. By G. Long, M.A. 2s. 6d.

Catullus, Tibullus, and Propertius. Selected Poems. With Life. By Rev. A. H. Wratislaw. 3s. 6d.

Cicero: De Senectute, De Amicitia, and Select Epistles. By
George Long, M.A. 4*s.* 6*d.*

Cornelius Nepos. By Rev. J. F. Macmichael. 2*s.* 6*d.*

Homer: Iliad. Books I.-XII. By F. A. Paley, M.A. 6*s.* 6*d.*

Horace. With Life. By A. J. Macleane, M.A. 6*s.* 6*d.* [In
2 parts. 3*s.* 6*d.* each.]

Juvenal: Sixteen Satires. By H. Prior, M.A. 4*s.* 6*d.*

Martial: Select Epigrams. With Life. By F. A. Paley, M.A. 6*s.* 6*d.*

Ovid: the Fasti. By F. A. Paley, M.A. 5*s.*

Sallust: Catilina and Jugurtha. With Life. By G. Long, M.A. 5*s.*

Tacitus: Germania and Agricola. By Rev. P. Frost. 3*s.* 6*d.*

Virgil: Bucolics, Georgics, and Æneid, Books I.-IV. Abridged
from Professor Conington's Edition. 5*s.* 6*d.*—Æneid, Books V.-XII. 5*s.* 6*d.*
Also in 9 separate Volumes, 1*s.* 6*d.* each.

Xenophon: The Anabasis. With Life. By Rev. J. F. Macmichael. 5*s.*
Also in 4 separate volumes, 1*s.* 6*d.* each.

———— The Cyropædia. By G. M. Gorham, M.A. 6*s.*

———— Memorabilia. By Percival Frost, M.A. 4*s.* 6*d.*

A Grammar-School Atlas of Classical Geography, containing
Ten selected Maps. Imperial 8vo. 5*s.*

Uniform with the Series.

The New Testament, in Greek. With English Notes, &c. By
Rev. J. F. Macmichael. 7*s.* 6*d.*

CAMBRIDGE GREEK AND LATIN TEXTS.

Æschylus. By F. A. Paley, M.A. 3*s.*

Cæsar: De Bello Gallico. By G. Long, M.A. 2*s.*

Cicero: De Senectute et de Amicitia, et Epistolæ Selectæ. By
G. Long, M.A. 1*s.* 6*d.*

Ciceronis Orationes. Vol. I. (in Verrem.) By G. Long, M.A. 3*s.* 6*d.*

Euripides. By F. A. Paley, M.A. 3 vols. 3*s.* 6*d.* each.

Herodotus. By J. G. Blakesley, B.D. 2 vols. 7*s.*

Homeri Ilias. I.-XII. By F. A. Paley, M.A. 2*s.* 6*d.*

Horatius. By A. J. Macleane, M.A. 2*s.* 6*d.*

Juvenal et Persius. By A. J. Macleane, M.A. 1*s.* 6*d.*

Lucretius. By H. A. J. Munro, M.A. 2*s.* 6*d.*

Sallusti Crispi Catilina et Jugurtha. By G. Long, M.A. 1*s.* 6*d.*

Sophocles. By F. A. Paley, M.A. 3*s.* 6*d.*

Terenti Comœdiæ. By W. Wagner, Ph.D. 3*s.*

Thucydides. By J. G. Donaldson, D.D. 2 vols. 7*s.*

Virgilius. By J. Conington, M.A. 3*s.* 6*d.*

Xenophontis Expeditio Cyri. By J. F. Macmichael, B.A. 2*s.* 6*d.*

Novum Testamentum Græcum. By F. H. Scrivener, M.A.
4*s.* 6*d.* An edition with wide margin for notes, half bound, 12*s.*

CAMBRIDGE TEXTS WITH NOTES.

A Selection of the most usually read of the Greek and Latin Authors,
Annotated for Schools. Fcap. 8vo. 1s. 6d. each, with exceptions.

Euripides. Alcestis.—Medea.—Hippolytus.—Hecuba.—Bacchæ.
Ion. 2s.—Orestes.—Phoenissæ.—Troades. By F. A. Paley, M.A.

Æschylus. Prometheus Vinctus.—Septem contra Thebas.—Agamemnon.—Persæ.—Eumenides. By F. A. Paley, M.A.

Sophocles. Œdipus Tyrannus.—Œdipus Coloneus.—Antigone.
By F. A. Paley, M.A.

Homer. Iliad. Book I. By F. A. Paley, M.A. 1s.

Terence. Andria.—Hauton Timorumenos.—Phormio.—Adelphoe.
By Professor Wagner, Ph.D.

Cicero's De Senectute, De Amicitia, and Epistolæ Selectæ. By
G. Long, M.A.

Ovid. Selections. By A. J. Macleane, M.A.
Others in preparation.

PUBLIC SCHOOL SERIES.

A Series of Classical Texts, annotated by well-known Scholars. Cr. 8vo.

Aristophanes. The Peace. By F. A. Paley, M.A. 4s. 6d.

———— The Acharnians. By F. A. Paley, M.A. 4s. 6d.

———— The Frogs. By F. A. Paley, M.A. 4s. 6d.

Cicero. The Letters to Atticus. Bk. I. By A. Pretor, M.A. 4s. 6d.

Demosthenes de Falsa Legatione. By R. Shilleto, M.A. 6s.

———— The Law of Leptines. By B. W. Beatson, M.A. 3s. 6d.

Plato. The Apology of Socrates and Crito. By W. Wagner, Ph.D.
7th Edition. 4s. 6d.

———— The Phædo. 6th Edition. By W. Wagner, Ph.D. 5s. 6d.

———— The Protagoras. 3rd Edition. By W. Wayte, M.A. 4s. 6d.

———— The Euthyphro. 2nd edition. By G. H. Wells, M.A. 3s.

———— The Euthydemus. By G. H. Wells, M.A. 4s.

———— The Republic. Books I. & II. By G. H. Wells, M.A. 5s. 6d.

Plautus. The Aulularia. By W. Wagner, Ph.D. 2nd edition. 4s. 6d.

———— Trinummus. By W. Wagner, Ph.D. 2nd edition. 4s. 6d.

———— The Menaechmei. By W. Wagner, Ph.D. 4s. 6d.

Sophoclis Trachiniæ. By A. Pretor, M.A. 4s. 6d.

Terence. By W. Wagner, Ph.D. 10s. 6d.

Theocritus. By F. A. Paley, M.A. 4s. 6d.
Others in preparation.

CRITICAL AND ANNOTATED EDITIONS.

Ætna. By H. A. J. Munro, M.A. 3s. 6d.

Aristophanis Comœdiæ. By H. A. Holden, LL.D. 8vo. 2 vols.
23s. 6d. Plays sold separately.

———— Pax. By F. A. Paley, M.A. Fcap. 8vo. 4s. 6d.

Catullus. By H. A. J. Munro, M.A. 7s. 6d.

Corpus Poetarum Latinorum. Edited by Walker. 1 vol. 8vo. 18s.

Horace. Quinti Horatii Flacci Opera. By H. A. J. Munro, M.A.
Large 8vo. 1l. 1s.

Livy. The first five Books. By J. Prendeville. 12mo. roan, 5s.
Or Books I.-III. 3s. 6d. IV. and V. 3s. 6d.

Lucretius. Titi Lucretii Cari de Rerum Natura Libri Sex. With a Translation and Notes. By H. A. J. Munro, M.A. 2 vols. 8vo. Vol. I. Text. (New Edition, Preparing.) Vol. II. Translation. (Sold separately.)

Ovid. P. Ovidii Nasonis Heroides XIV. By A. Palmer, M.A. 8vo. 6*s.*

Propertius. Sex Aurelii Propertii Carmina. By F. A. Paley, M.A. 8vo. Cloth, 9*s.*

Sex. Propertii Elegiarum. Lib. IV. By A. Palmer. Fcap. 8vo. 5*s.*

Sophocles. The Ajax. By C. E. Palmer, M.A. 4*s.* 6*d.*

Thucydides. The History of the Peloponnesian War. By Richard Shilleto, M.A. Book I. 8vo. 6*s.* 6*d.* Book II. 8vo. 5*s.* 6*d.*

LATIN AND GREEK CLASS-BOOKS.

Auxilia Latina. A Series of Progressive Latin Exercises. By M. J. B. Baddeley, M.A. Fcap. 8vo. Part I. Accidence. 2nd Edition, revised. 1*s.* 6*d.* Part II. 4th Edition, revised. 2*s.* Key to Part II. 2*s.* 6*d.*

Latin Prose Lessons. By Prof. Church, M.A. 6th Edit. Fcap. 8vo. 2*s.* 6*d.*

Latin Exercises and Grammar Papers. By T. Collins, M.A. 3rd Edition. Fcap. 8vo. 2*s.* 6*d.*

Unseen Papers in Latin Prose and Verse. With Examination Questions. By T. Collins, M.A. 2nd Edition. Fcap. 8vo. 2*s.* 6*d.*

—— in Greek Prose and Verse. With Examination Questions. By T. Collins, M.A. Fcap. 8vo. 3*s.*

Analytical Latin Exercises. By C. P. Mason, B.A. 3rd Edit. 3*s.* 6*d.*

Latin Mood Construction, Outlines of. With Exercises. By the Rev. G. E. C. Casey, M.A., F.L.S., F.G.S. Small post 8vo. 1*s.* 6*d.* Latin of the Exercises. 1*s.* 6*d.*

Scala Græca: a Series of Elementary Greek Exercises. By Rev. J. W. Davis, M.A., and R. W. Baddeley, M.A. 3rd Edition. Fcap. 8vo. 2*s.* 6*d.*

Greek Verse Composition. By G. Preston, M.A. Crown 8vo. 4*s.* 6*d.*

Greek Particles and their Combinations according to Attic Usage. A Short Treatise. By F. A. Paley, M.A. 2*s.* 6*d.*

BY THE REV. P. FROST, M.A., ST. JOHN'S COLLEGE, CAMBRIDGE.

Eclogæ Latinæ; or, First Latin Reading-Book, with English Notes and a Dictionary. New Edition. Fcap. 8vo. 2*s.* 6*d.*

Materials for Latin Prose Composition. New Edition. Fcap. 8vo. 2*s.* 6*d.* Key, 4*s.*

A Latin Verse-Book. An Introductory Work on Hexameters and Pentameters. New Edition. Fcap. 8vo. 3*s.* Key, 5*s.*

Analecta Græca Minora, with Introductory Sentences, English Notes, and a Dictionary. New Edition. Fcap. 8vo. 3*s.* 6*d.*

Materials for Greek Prose Composition. New Edit. Fcap. 8vo. 3*s.* 6*d.* Key, 5*s.*

Florilegium Poeticum. Elegiac Extracts from Ovid and Tibullus. New Edition. With Notes. Fcap. 8vo. 3*s.*

BY THE REV. F. E. GRETTON.

A First Cheque-book for Latin Verse-makers. 1*s.* 6*d.*

A Latin Version for Masters. 2*s.* 6*d.*

Reddenda; or Passages with Parallel Hints for Translation into Latin Prose and Verse. Crown 8vo. 4*s.* 6*d.*

Reddenda Reddita (*see next page*).

By H. A. HOLDEN, LL.D.

Foliorum Silvula. Part I. Passages for Translation into Latin Elegiac and Heroic Verse. 9th Edition. Post 8vo. 7s. 6d.

—— Part II. Select Passages for Translation into Latin Lyric and Comic Iambic Verse. 3rd Edition. Post 8vo. 5s.

—— Part III. Select Passages for Translation into Greek Verse. 3rd Edition. Post 8vo. 8s.

Folia Silvulæ, sive Eclogæ Poetarum Anglicorum in Latinum et Græcum conversæ. 8vo. Vol. I. 10s. 6d. Vol. II. 12s.

Foliorum Centuriæ. Select Passages for Translation into Latin and Greek Prose. 7th Edition. Post 8vo. 8s.

TRANSLATIONS, SELECTIONS, &c.

*** Many of the following books are well adapted for School Prizes.

Æschylus. Translated into English Prose by F. A. Paley, M.A. 2nd Edition. 8vo. 7s. 6d.

—— Translated into English Verse by Anna Swanwick. Post 8vo. 5s.

Anthologia Græca. A Selection of Choice Greek Poetry, with Notes. By F. St. John Thackeray. 4th and Cheaper Edition. 16mo. 4s. 6d.

Anthologia Latina. A Selection of Choice Latin Poetry, from Nævius to Boëthius, with Notes. By Rev. F. St. John Thackeray. Revised and Cheaper Edition. 16mo. 4s. 6d.

Horace. The Odes and Carmen Sæculare. In English Verse by J. Conington, M.A. 8th edition. Fcap. 8vo. 5s. 6d.

—— The Satires and Epistles. In English Verse by J. Conington, M.A. 5th edition. 6s. 6d.

—— Illustrated from Antique Gems by C. W. King, M.A. The text revised with Introduction by H. A. J. Munro, M.A. Large 8vo. 1l. 1s.

Horace's Odes. Englished and Imitated by various hands. Edited by C. W. F. Cooper. Crown 8vo. 6s. 6d.

Propertius. Verse Translations from Book V., with revised Latin Text. By F. A. Paley, M.A. Fcap. 8vo. 3s.

Plato. Gorgias. Translated by E. M. Cope, M.A. 8vo. 7s.

—— Philebus. Translated by F. A. Paley, M.A. Small 8vo. 4s.

—— Theætetus. Translated by F. A. Paley, M.A. Small 8vo. 4s.

—— Analysis and Index of the Dialogues. By Dr. Day. Post 8vo. 5s.

Reddenda Reddita : Passages from English Poetry, with a Latin Verse Translation. By F. E. Gretton. Crown 8vo. 6s.

Sabrinæ Corolla in hortulis Regiæ Scholæ Salopiensis contexuerunt tres viri floribus legendis. Editio tertia. 8vo. 8s. 6d.

Theocritus. In English Verse, by C. S. Calverley, M.A. Crown 8vo. [New Edition preparing.

Translations into English and Latin. By C. S. Calverley, M.A. Post 8vo. 7s. 6d.

—— into Greek and Latin Verse. By R. C. Jebb. 4to. cloth gilt. 10s. 6d.

Between Whiles. Translations by B. H. Kennedy. 2nd Edition. revised. Crown 8vo. 6s.

REFERENCE VOLUMES.

A Latin Grammar. By Albert Harkness. Post 8vo. 6*s.*

——— By T. H. Key, M.A. 6th Thousand. Post 8vo. 8*s.*

A Short Latin Grammar for Schools. By T. H. Key, M.A., F.R.S. 14th Edition. Post 8vo. 3*s.* 6*d.*

A Guide to the Choice of Classical Books. By J. B. Mayor, M.A. Revised Edition. Crown 8vo. 3*s.*

The Theatre of the Greeks. By J. W. Donaldson, D.D. 8th Edition. Post 8vo. 5*s.*

Keightley's Mythology of Greece and Italy. 4th Edition. 5*s.*

A Dictionary of Latin and Greek Quotations. By H. T. Riley. Post 8vo. 5*s.* With Index Verborum, 6*s.*

A History of Roman Literature. By W. S. Teuffel, Professor at the University of Tübingen. By W. Wagner, Ph.D. 2 vols. Demy 8vo. 21*s.*

Student's Guide to the University of Cambridge. 4th Edition revised. Fcap. 8vo. Part 1, 2*s.* 6*d.* ; Parts 2 to 6, 1*s.* each.

CLASSICAL TABLES.

Latin Accidence. By the Rev. P. Frost, M.A. 1*s.*

Latin Versification. 1*s.*

Notabilia Quædam ; or the Principal Tenses of most of the Irregular Greek Verbs and Elementary Greek, Latin, and French Construction. New Edition. 1*s.*

Richmond Rules for the Ovidian Distich, &c. By J. Tate, M.A. 1*s.*

The Principles of Latin Syntax. 1*s.*

Greek Verbs. A Catalogue of Verbs, Irregular and Defective; their leading formations, tenses, and inflexions, with Paradigms for conjugation, Rules for formation of tenses, &c. &c. By J. S. Baird, T.C.D. 2*s.* 6*d.*

Greek Accents (Notes on). By A. Barry, D.D. New Edition. 1*s.*

Homeric Dialect. Its Leading Forms and Peculiarities. By J. S. Baird, T.C.D. New Edition, by W. G. Rutherford. 1*s.*

Greek Accidence. By the Rev. P. Frost, M.A. New Edition. 1*s.*

CAMBRIDGE MATHEMATICAL SERIES.

Algebra. Choice and Chance. By W. A. Whitworth, M.A. 3rd Edition. 6*s.*

Euclid. Exercises on Euclid and in Modern Geometry. By J. McDowell, M.A. 3rd Edition. 6*s.*

Trigonometry. Plane. By Rev. T. Vyvyan, M.A. 3*s.* 6*d.*

Conics. The Geometry of. By C. Taylor, D.D. 4*s.* 6*d.*

Solid Geometry. By W. S. Aldis, M.A. 3rd Edition. 6*s.*

Rigid Dynamics. By W. S. Aldis, M.A. 4*s.*

Elementary Dynamics. By W. Garnett, M.A. 3rd Edition. 6*s.*

Heat. An Elementary Treatise. By W. Garnett, M.A. 2nd Edit.
3s. 6d.

Hydromechanics. By W. H. Besant, M.A., F.R.S. 4th Edition.
[*In the press.*

Mechanics. Problems in Elementary. By W. Walton, M.A. 6s.

CAMBRIDGE SCHOOL AND COLLEGE TEXT-BOOKS.

A Series of Elementary Treatises for the use of Students in the Universities, Schools, and Candidates for the Public Examinations. Fcap. 8vo.

Arithmetic. By Rev. C. Elsee, M.A. Fcap. 8vo. 10th Edit. 3s. 6d.

Algebra. By the Rev. C. Elsee, M.A. 6th Edit. 4s.

Arithmetic. By A. Wrigley, M.A. 3s. 6d.

—— A Progressive Course of Examples. With Answers. By
J. Watson, M.A. 5th Edition. 2s. 6d.

Algebra. Progressive Course of Examples. By Rev. W. F.
M'Michael, M.A., and R. Prowde Smith, M.A. 2nd Edition. 3s. 6d. With
Answers. 4s. 6d.

Plane Astronomy, An Introduction to. By P. T. Main, M.A.
4th Edition. 4s.

Conic Sections treated Geometrically. By W. H. Besant, M.A.
4th Edition. 4s. 6d. Solution to the Examples. 4s.

Elementary Conic Sections treated Geometrically. By W. H.
Besant, M.A. [*In the Press.*

Statics, Elementary. By Rev. H. Goodwin, D.D. 2nd Edit. 3s.

Hydrostatics, Elementary. By W. H. Besant, M.A. 10th Edit. 4s.

Mensuration, An Elementary Treatise on. By B. T. Moore, M.A. 6s.

Newton's Principia, The First Three Sections of, with an Appendix; and the Ninth and Eleventh Sections. By J. H. Evans, M.A. 5th
Edition, by P. T. Main, M.A. 4s.

Trigonometry, Elementary. By T. P. Hudson, M.A. 3s. 6d.

Optics, Geometrical. With Answers. By W. S. Aldis, M.A. 3s. 6d.

Analytical Geometry for Schools. By T. G. Vyvyan. 3rd Edit. 4s. 6d.

Greek Testament, Companion to the. By A. C. Barrett, A.M.
4th Edition, revised. Fcap. 8vo. 5s.

Book of Common Prayer, An Historical and Explanatory Treatise
on the. By W. G. Humphry, B.D. 6th Edition. Fcap. 8vo. 4s. 6d.

Music, Text-book of. By H. C. Banister. 10th Edit. revised. 5s.

—— Concise History of. By Rev. H. G. Bonavia Hunt, B. Mus.
Oxon. 5th Edition revised. 3s. 6d.

ARITHMETIC AND ALGEBRA.
See foregoing Series.

GEOMETRY AND EUCLID.

Euclid. The First Two Books explained to Beginners. By C. P. Mason, B.A. 2nd Edition. Fcap 8vo. 2s. 6d.

The Enunciations and Figures to Euclid's Elements. By Rev. J. Brasse, D.D. New Edition. Fcap. 8vo. 1s. On Cards, in case, 5s. 6d. Without the Figures, 6d.

Exercises on Euclid and in Modern Geometry. By J. McDowell, B.A. Crown 8vo. 3rd Edition revised. 6s.

Geometrical Conic Sections. By W. H. Besant, M.A. 4th Edit. 4s. 6d. Solution to the Examples. 4s.

Elementary Geometrical Conic Sections. By W. H. Besant, M.A. [In the press.

Elementary Geometry of Conics. By C. Taylor, D.D. 3rd Edit. 8vo. 4s. 6d.

An Introduction to Ancient and Modern Geometry of Conics. By C. Taylor, M.A. 8vo. 15s.

Solutions of Geometrical Problems, proposed at St. John's College from 1830 to 1846. By T. Gaskin, M.A. 8vo. 12s.

TRIGONOMETRY.

Trigonometry, Introduction to Plane. By Rev. T. G. Vyvyan, Charterhouse. Cr. 8vo. 3s. 6d.

Elementary Trigonometry. By T. P. Hudson, M.A. 3s. 6d.

An Elementary Treatise on Mensuration. By B. T. Moore, M.A. 5s.

ANALYTICAL GEOMETRY
AND DIFFERENTIAL CALCULUS.

An Introduction to Analytical Plane Geometry. By W. P. Turnbull, M.A. 8vo. 12s.

Problems on the Principles of Plane Co-ordinate Geometry. By W. Walton, M.A. 8vo. 16s.

Trilinear Co-ordinates, and Modern Analytical Geometry of Two Dimensions. By W. A. Whitworth, M.A. 8vo. 16s.

An Elementary Treatise on Solid Geometry. By W. S. Aldis, M.A. 2nd Edition revised. 8vo. 8s.

Elementary Treatise on the Differential Calculus. By M. O'Brien, M.A. 8vo. 10s. 6d.

Elliptic Functions, Elementary Treatise on. By A. Cayley, M.A. Demy 8vo. 15s.

MECHANICS & NATURAL PHILOSOPHY.

Statics, Elementary. By H. Goodwin, D.D. Fcap. 8vo. 2nd Edition. 3s.

Dynamics, A Treatise on Elementary. By W. Garnett, M.A. 3rd Edition. Crown 8vo. 6s.

Elementary Mechanics, Problems in. By W. Walton, M.A. New Edition. Crown 8vo. 6s.

Theoretical Mechanics, Problems in. By W. Walton. 2nd Edit. revised and enlarged. Demy 8vo. 16s.

Hydrostatics. By W. H. Besant, M.A. Fcap. 8vo. 10th Edition. **4s.**

Hydromechanics, A Treatise on. By W. H. Besant, M.A., F.R.S.
8vo. 4th Edition, revised. [*Immediately.*

Dynamics of a Particle, A Treatise on the. By W. H. Besant, M.A.
[*Preparing.*

Optics, Geometrical. By W. S. Aldis, M.A. Fcap. 8vo. **3s. 6d.**

Double Refraction, A Chapter on Fresnel's Theory of. By W. S.
Aldis, M.A. 8vo. 2s.

Heat, An Elementary Treatise on. By W. Garnett, M.A. Crown
8vo. 2nd Edition revised. 3s. 6d.

Newton's Principia, The First Three Sections of, with an Appendix; and the Ninth and Eleventh Sections. By J. H. Evans, M.A. 5th
Edition. Edited by P. T. Main, M.A. 4s.

Astronomy, An Introduction to Plane. By P. T. Main, M.A.
Fcap. 8vo. cloth. 4s.

Astronomy, Practical and Spherical. By R. Main, M.A. 8vo. **14s.**

Astronomy, Elementary Chapters on, from the 'Astronomie
Physique' of Biot. By H. Goodwin, D.D. 8vo. 3s. 6d.

Pure Mathematics and Natural Philosophy, A Compendium of
Facts and Formulæ in. By G. R. Smalley. 2nd Edition, revised by
J. McDowell, M.A. Fcap. 8vo. 3s. 6d.

Elementary Course of Mathematics. By H. Goodwin, D.D.
6th Edition. 8vo. 16s.

Problems and Examples, adapted to the 'Elementary Course of
Mathematics.' 3rd Edition. 8vo. 5s.

Solutions of Goodwin's Collection of Problems and Examples.
By W. W. Hutt, M.A. 3rd Edition, revised and enlarged. 8vo. 9s.

Pure Mathematics, Elementary Examples in. By J. Taylor. 8vo.
7s. 6d.

Mechanics of Construction. With numerous Examples. By
S. Fenwick, F.R.A.S. 8vo. 12s.

Pure and Applied Calculation, Notes on the Principles of. By
Rev. J. Challis, M.A. Demy 8vo. 15s.

Physics, The Mathematical Principle of. By Rev. J. Challis, M.A.
Demy 8vo. 5s.

TECHNOLOGICAL HANDBOOKS.

Edited by H. Trueman Wood, Secretary of the
Society of Arts.

1. Dyeing and Tissue Printing. By W. Crookes, F.R.S.
[*In the press.*

2. Glass Manufacture. By Henry Chance, M.A.; H. J. Powell, B.A.;
and H. G. Harris. [*Immediately.*

3. Cotton Manufacture. By Richard Marsden, Esq., of Man-
chester. [*Preparing.*

4. Telegraphs and Telephones. By W. H. Preece, F.R.S.
[*Preparing.*

5. Iron and Steel. By Prof. A. K. Huntington, of King's College.
[*Preparing.*

HISTORY, TOPOGRAPHY, &c.

Rome and the Campagna. By R. Burn, M.A. With 85 Engravings and 26 Maps and Plans. With Appendix. 4to. 3*l*. 3*s*.

Old Rome. A Handbook for Travellers. By R. Burn, M.A. With Maps and Plans. Demy 8vo. 10*s*. 6*d*.

Modern Europe. By Dr. T. H. Dyer. 2nd Edition, revised and continued. 5 vols. Demy 8vo. 2*l*. 12*s*. 6*d*.

The History of the Kings of Rome. By Dr. T. H. Dyer. 8vo. 16*s*.

The History of Pompeii: its Buildings and Antiquities. By T. H. Dyer. 3rd Edition, brought down to 1874. Post 8vo. 7*s*. 6*d*.

Ancient Athens: its History, Topography, and Remains. By T. H. Dyer. Super-royal 8vo. Cloth. 1*l*. 5*s*.

The Decline of the Roman Republic. By G. Long. 5 vols. 8vo. 14*s*. each.

A History of England during the Early and Middle Ages. By C. H. Pearson, M.A. 2nd Edition revised and enlarged. 8vo. Vol. I. 16*s*. Vol. II. 14*s*.

Historical Maps of England. By C. H. Pearson. Folio. 2nd Edition revised. 31*s*. 6*d*.

History of England, 1800–15. By Harriet Martineau, with new and copious Index. 1 vol. 3*s*. 6*d*.

History of the Thirty Years' Peace, 1815–46. By Harriet Martineau. 4 vols. 3*s*. 6*d*. each.

A Practical Synopsis of English History. By A. Bowes. 4th Edition. 8vo. 2*s*.

Student's Text-Book of English and General History. By D. Beale. Crown 8vo. 2*s*. 6*d*.

Lives of the Queens of England. By A. Strickland. Library Edition, 8 vols. 7*s*. 6*d*. each. Cheaper Edition, 6 vols. 5*s*. each. Abridged Edition, 1 vol. 6*s*. 6*d*.

Eginhard's Life of Karl the Great (Charlemagne). Translated with Notes, by W. Glaister, M.A., B.C.L. Crown 8vo. 4*s*. 6*d*.

Outlines of Indian History. By A. W. Hughes. Small post 8vo. 3*s*. 6*d*.

The Elements of General History. By Prof. Tytler. New Edition, brought down to 1874. Small post 8vo. 3*s*. 6*d*.

ATLASES.

An Atlas of Classical Geography. 24 Maps. By W. Hughes and G. Long, M.A. New Edition. Imperial 8vo. 12*s*. 6*d*.

A Grammar-School Atlas of Classical Geography. Ten Maps selected from the above. New Edition. Imperial 8vo. 5*s*.

First Classical Maps. By the Rev. J. Tate, M.A. 3rd Edition. Imperial 8vo. 7*s*. 6*d*.

Standard Library Atlas of Classical Geography. Imp. 8vo. 7*s*. 6*d*.

PHILOLOGY.

WEBSTER'S DICTIONARY OF THE ENGLISH LAN-GUAGE. With Dr. Mahn's Etymology. 1 vol., 1628 Pages, 3000 Illustrations. 21*s.* With Appendices and 70 additional pages of Illustrations, 1919 Pages, 31*s.* 6*d.*
'THE BEST PRACTICAL ENGLISH DICTIONARY EXTANT.'—*Quarterly Review,*1873.
Prospectuses, with specimen pages, post free on application.

New Dictionary of the English Language. Combining Explanation with Etymology, and copiously illustrated by Quotations from the best Authorities. By Dr. Richardson. New Edition, with a Supplement. 2 vols. 4to. 4*l.* 14*s.* 6*d.*; half russia, 5*l.* 15*s.* 6*d.*; russia, 6*l.* 12*s.* Supplement separately. 4to. 12*s.*
An 8vo. Edit. without the Quotations, 15*s.*; half russia, 20*s.*; russia, 24*s.*

Supplementary English Glossary. Containing 12,000 Words and Meanings occurring in English Literature, not found in any other Dictionary. By T. L. O. Davies. Demy 8vo. 16*s.*

Folk-Etymology. A Dictionary of Corrupted Words. By Rev. A. S. Palmer. [*Immediately.*

Brief History of the English Language. By Prof. James Hadley, LL.D., Yale College. Fcap. 8vo. 1*s.*

The Elements of the English Language. By E. Adams, Ph.D. 15th Edition. Post 8vo. 4*s.* 6*d.*

Philological Essays. By T. H. Key, M.A., F.R.S. 8vo. 10*s.* 6*d.*

Language, its Origin and Development. By T. H. Key, M.A., F.R.S. 8vo. 14*s.*

Synonyms and Antonyms of the English Language. By Archdeacon Smith. 2nd Edition. Post 8vo. 5*s.*

Synonyms Discriminated. By Archdeacon Smith. Demy 8vo. 16*s.*

Bible English. By T. L. O. Davies. 5*s.*

The Queen's English. A Manual of Idiom and Usage. By the late Dean Alford 6th Edition. Fcap. 8vo. 5*s.*

Etymological Glossary of nearly 2500 English Words derived from the Greek. By the Rev. E. J. Boyce. Fcap. 8vo. 3*s.* 6*d.*

A Syriac Grammar. By G. Phillips, D.D. 3rd Edition, enlarged. 8vo. 7*s.* 6*d.*

A Grammar of the Arabic Language. By Rev. W. J. Beaumont, M.A. 12mo. 7*s.*

DIVINITY, MORAL PHILOSOPHY, &c.

Novum Testamentum Græcum, Textus Stephanici, 1550. By F. H. Scrivener, A.M., LL.D., D.C.L. New Edition. 16mo. 4*s.* 6*d.* Also on Writing Paper, with Wide Margin. Half-bound. 12*s.*

By the same Author.

Codex Bezæ Cantabrigiensis. 4to. 26*s.*

A Full Collation of the Codex Sinaiticus with the Received Text of the New Testament, with Critical Introduction. 2nd Edition, revised. Fcap. 8vo. 5*s.*

A Plain Introduction to the Criticism of the New Testament. With Forty Facsimiles from Ancient Manuscripts. 3rd Edition. 8vo. [*In the press.*

Six Lectures on the Text of the New Testament. For English Readers. Crown 8vo. 6*s.*

The New Testament for English Readers. By the late H. Alford,
D.D. Vol. I. Part I. 3rd Edit. 12s. Vol. I. Part II. 2nd Edit. 10s. 6d.
Vol. II. Part I. 2nd Edit. 16s. Vol. II. Part II. 2nd Edit. 16s.

The Greek Testament. By the late H. Alford, D.D. Vol. I. 6th
Edit. 1l. 8s. Vol. II. 6th Edit. 1l. 4s. Vol. III. 5th Edit. 18s. Vol. IV.
Part I. 4th Edit. 18s. Vol. IV. Part II. 4th Edit. 14s. Vol. IV. 1l. 12s.

Companion to the Greek Testament. By A. C. Barrett, M.A.
4th Edition, revised. Fcap. 8vo. 5s.

The Book of Psalms. A New Translation, with Introductions, &c.
By the Very Rev. J. J. Stewart Perowne, D.D. 8vo. Vol. I. 5th Edition,
18s. Vol. II. 5th Edit. 16s.

—— Abridged for Schools. 3rd Edition. Crown 8vo. 10s. 6d.

History of the Articles of Religion. By C. H. Hardwick. 3rd
Edition. Post 8vo. 5s.

History of the Creeds. By J. R. Lumby, D.D. 2nd Edition.
Crown 8vo. 7s. 6d.

Pearson on the Creed. Carefully printed from an early edition.
With Analysis and Index by E. Walford, M.A. Post 8vo. 5s.

**An Historical and Explanatory Treatise on the Book of
Common Prayer.** By Rev. W. G. Humphry, B.D. 6th Edition, enlarged.
Small post 8vo. 4s. 6d.

The New Table of Lessons Explained. By Rev. W. G. Humphry,
B.D. Fcap. 1s. 6d.

A Commentary on the Gospels for the Sundays and other Holy
Days of the Christian Year. By Rev. W. Denton, A.M. New Edition.
3 vols. 8vo. 54s. Sold separately.

Commentary on the Epistles for the Sundays and other Holy
Days of the Christian Year. By Rev. W. Denton, A.M. 2 vols. 36s. Sold
separately.

Commentary on the Acts. By Rev. W. Denton, A.M. Vol. I.
8vo. 18s. Vol. II. 14s.

Notes on the Catechism. By Rev. Canon Barry, D.D. 6th Edit.
Fcap. 2s.

Catechetical Hints and Helps. By Rev. E. J. Boyce, M.A. 4th
Edition, revised. Fcap. 2s. 6d.

Examination Papers on Religious Instruction. By Rev. E. J.
Boyce. Sewed. 1s. 6d.

Church Teaching for the Church's Children. An Exposition
of the Catechism. By the Rev. F. W. Harper. Sq. fcap. 2s.

The Winton Church Catechist. Questions and Answers on the
Teaching of the Church Catechism. By the late Rev. J. S. B. Monsell,
LL.D. 3rd Edition. Cloth, 3s.; or in Four Parts, sewed.

The Church Teacher's Manual of Christian Instruction. By
Rev. M. F. Sadler. 21st Thousand. 2s. 6d.

**Short Explanation of the Epistles and Gospels of the Chris-
tian Year,** with Questions. Royal 32mo. 2s. 6d.; calf, 4s. 6d.

Butler's Analogy of Religion; with Introduction and Index by
Rev. Dr. Steere. New Edition. Fcap. 3s. 6d.

—— **Three Sermons on Human Nature, and Dissertation on**
Virtue. By W. Whewell, D.D. 4th Edition. Fcap. 8vo. 2s. 6d.

Lectures on the History of Moral Philosophy in England. By W. Whewell, D.D. Crown 8vo. 8s.

Kent's Commentary on International Law. By J. T. Abdy, LL.D. New and Cheap Edition. Crown 8vo. 10s. 6d.

A Manual of the Roman Civil Law. By G. Leapingwell, LL.D. 8vo. 12s.

FOREIGN CLASSICS.

A series for use in Schools, with English Notes, grammatical and explanatory, and renderings of difficult idiomatic expressions. Fcap. 8vo.

Schiller's Wallenstein. By Dr. A. Buchheim. 3rd Edit. 6s. 6d. Or the Lager and Piccolomini, 3s. 6d. Wallenstein's Tod, 3s. 6d.

—— Maid of Orleans. By Dr. W. Wagner. 3s. 6d.

—— Maria Stuart. By V. Kastner. 3s.

Goethe's Hermann and Dorothea. By E. Bell, M.A., and E. Wölfel. 2s. 6d.

German Ballads, from Uhland, Goethe, and Schiller. By C. L. Bielefeld. 3rd Edition. 3s. 6d.

Charles XII., par Voltaire. By L. Direy. 4th Edition. 3s. 6d.

Aventures de Télémaque, par Fénélon. By C. J. Delille. 2nd Edition. 4s. 6d.

Select Fables of La Fontaine. By F. E. A. Gasc. 14th Edition. 3s.

Picciola, by X. B. Saintine. By Dr. Dubuc. 11th Thousand. 3s. 6d.

FRENCH CLASS-BOOKS.

Twenty Lessons in French. With Vocabulary, giving the Pronunciation. By W. Brebner. Post 8vo. 4s.

French Grammar for Public Schools. By Rev. A. C. Clapin, M.A. Fcap. 8vo. 9th Edition, revised. 2s. 6d.

French Primer. By Rev. A. C. Clapin, M.A. Fcap. 8vo. 4th Edit. 1s.

Primer of French Philology. By Rev. A. C. Clapin. Fcap. 8vo. 1s.

Le Nouveau Trésor; or, French Student's Companion. By M. E. S. 16th Edition. Fcap. 8vo. 3s. 6d.

F. E. A. GASC'S FRENCH COURSE.

First French Book. Fcap. 8vo. 76th Thousand. 1s. 6d.

Second French Book. 37th Thousand. Fcap. 8vo. 2s. 6d.

Key to First and Second French Books. Fcap. 8vo. 3s. 6d.

French Fables for Beginners, in Prose, with Index. 14th Thousand. 12mo. 2s.

Select Fables of La Fontaine. New Edition. Fcap. 8vo. 3s.

Histoires Amusantes et Instructives. With Notes. 14th Thousand. Fcap. 8vo. 2s. 6d.

Practical Guide to Modern French Conversation. 12th Thousand. Fcap. 8vo. 2*s.* 6*d.*

French Poetry for the Young. With Notes. 4th Edition. Fcap. 8vo. 2*s.*

Materials for French Prose Composition; or, Selections from the best English Prose Writers. 16th Thousand. Fcap. 8vo. 4*s.* 6*d.* Key, 6*s.*

Prosateurs Contemporains. With Notes. 8vo. 6th Edition, revised. 5*s.*

Le Petit Compagnon; a French Talk-Book for Little Children. 10th Thousand. 16mo. 2*s.* 6*d.*

An Improved Modern Pocket Dictionary of the French and English Languages. 30th Thousand, with Additions. 16mo. Cloth. 4*s.* Also in 2 vols., in neat leatherette, 5*s.*

Modern French-English and English-French Dictionary. 2nd Edition, revised. In 1 vol. 12*s.* 6*d.* (formerly 2 vols. 25*s.*)

GOMBERT'S FRENCH DRAMA.

Being a Selection of the best Tragedies and Comedies of Molière, Racine, Corneille, and Voltaire. With Arguments and Notes by A. Gombert. New Edition, revised by F. E. A. Gasc. Fcap. 8vo. 1*s.* each; sewed, 6*d.*   CONTENTS.

MOLIERE:—Le Misanthrope. L'Avare. Le Bourgeois Gentilhomme. Le Tartuffe. Le Malade Imaginaire. Les Femmes Savantes. Les Fourberies de Scapin. Les Précieuses Ridicules. L'Ecole des Femmes. L'Ecole des Maris. Le Médecin malgré Lui.

RACINE:—Phèdre. Esther. Athalie. Iphigénie. Les Plaideurs. La Thébaïde; or, Les Frères Ennemis. Andromaque. Britannicus.

P. CORNEILLE:—Le Cid. Horace. Cinna. Polyeucte.

VOLTAIRE:—Zaïre.

GERMAN CLASS-BOOKS.

Materials for German Prose Composition. By Dr Buchheim. 7th Edition Fcap. 4*s.* 6*d.* Key, 3*s.*

A German Grammar for Public Schools. By the Rev. A. C. Clapin and F. Holl Müller. 2nd Edition. Fcap. 2*s.* 6*d.*

Kotzebue's Der Gefangene. With Notes by Dr. W. Stromberg. 1*s.*

ENGLISH CLASS-BOOKS.

A Brief History of the English Language. By Prof. Jas. Hadley, LL.D., of Yale College. Fcap. 8vo. 1*s.*

The Elements of the English Language. By E. Adams, Ph.D. 18th Edition. Post 8vo. 4*s.* 6*d.*

The Rudiments of English Grammar and Analysis. By E. Adams, Ph.D. 6th Edition. Fcap. 8vo. 2*s.*

By C. P. Mason, Fellow of Univ. Coll. London.

First Notions of Grammar for Young Learners. Fcap. 8vo.
10th Thousand. Cloth. 8d.

First Steps in English Grammar for Junior Classes. Demy
18mo. 32nd Thousand. 1s.

Outlines of English Grammar for the use of Junior Classes.
31st Thousand. Crown 8vo. 2s.

English Grammar, including the Principles of Grammatical
Analysis. 25th Edition. 86th Thousand. Crown 8vo. 3s. 6d.

A Shorter English Grammar, with copious Exercises. 8th Thousand. Crown 8vo. 3s. 6d.

English Grammar Practice, being the Exercises separately. 1s.

Practical Hints on Teaching. By Rev. J. Menet, M.A. 5th Edit.
Crown 8vo. cloth, 2s. 6d. ; paper, 2s.

Test Lessons in Dictation. 2nd Edition. Paper cover, 1s. 6d.

Questions for Examinations in English Literature. By Rev.
W. W. Skeat, Prof. of Anglo-Saxon at Cambridge University. 2s. 6d.

Drawing Copies. By P. H. Delamotte. Oblong 8vo. 12s. Sold
also in parts at 1s. each.

Poetry for the School-room. New Edition. Fcap. 8vo. 1s. 6d.

Geographical Text-Book; a Practical Geography. By M. E. S.
12mo. 2s.
  The Blank Maps done up separately, 4to. 2s. coloured.

Loudon's (Mrs.) Entertaining Naturalist. New Edition. Revised
by W. S. Dallas, F.L.S. 5s.

—— **Handbook of Botany.** New Edition, greatly enlarged by
D. Wooster. Fcap. 2s. 6d.

The Botanist's Pocket-Book. With a copious Index. By W. R.
Hayward. 3rd Edit. revised. Crown 8vo. Cloth limp. 4s. 6d.

Experimental Chemistry, founded on the Work of Dr. Stöckhardt.
By C. W. Heaton. Post 8vo. 5s.

Double Entry Elucidated. By B. W. Foster. 12th Edit. 4to.
3s. 6d.

A New Manual of Book-keeping. By P. Crellin, Accountant.
Crown 8vo. 3s. 6d.

Picture School-Books. In Simple Language, with numerous
Illustrations. Royal 16mo.

School Primer. 6d.—School Reader. By J. Tilleard. 1s.—Poetry Book
for Schools. 1s.—The Life of Joseph. 1s.—The Scripture Parables. By the
Rev. J. E. Clarke. 1s.—The Scripture Miracles. By the Rev. J. E. Clarke.
1s.—The New Testament History. By the Rev. J. G. Wood, M.A. 1s.—The
Old Testament History. By the Rev. J. G. Wood, M.A. 1s.—The Story of
Bunyan's Pilgrim's Progress. 1s.—The Life of Christopher Columbus. By
Sarah Crompton. 1s.—The Life of Martin Luther. By Sarah Crompton. 1s.

BOOKS FOR YOUNG READERS.

A Series of Reading Books designed to facilitate the acquisition of the power of Reading by very young Children. In 8 vols. limp cloth, 8d. each.

The Cat and the Hen.   Sam and his Dog Redleg. ⎫
  Bob and Tom Lee.   A Wreck.   ⎬ *Suitable*
The New-born Lamb.   The Rosewood Box.   Poor ⎪   *for*
  Fan.   Sheep Dog.   ⎭ *Infants.*

The Story of Three Monkeys. ⎫
Story of a Cat.   Told by Herself. ⎪
The Blind Boy.   The Mute Girl.   A New Tale of ⎪
  Babes in a Wood.   ⎪ *Suitable*
The Dey and the Knight.   The New Bank Note. ⎬   *for*
  The Royal Visit.   A King's Walk on a Winter's Day. ⎪ *Standards*
Queen Bee and Busy Bee.   ⎪ *I. and II.*
Gull's Cragg. ⎪
A First Book of Geography.   By the Rev. C. A. Johns. ⎪
  Illustrated.   Double size, 1s. ⎭

BELL'S READING-BOOKS.

FOR SCHOOLS AND PAROCHIAL LIBRARIES.

The popularity which the 'Books for Young Readers' have attained is a sufficient proof that teachers and pupils alike approve of the use of interesting stories, with a simple plot in place of the dry combination of letters and syllables, making no impression on the mind, of which elementary reading-books generally consist.

The Publishers have therefore thought it advisable to extend the application of this principle to books adapted for more advanced readers.

Now Ready.   Post 8vo.   Strongly bound.

Grimm's German Tales.   (Selected.)   1s. ⎫
Andersen's Danish Tales.   (Selected.)   1s. ⎬ *Suitable for*
Great Englishmen.   Short Lives for Young Children.   1s. ⎪ *Standards*
Edgeworth's Tales.   A Selection.   1s. ⎭ *II. & III.*

Friends in Fur and Feathers.   By Gwynfryn.   1s. ⎫
Parables from Nature.   (Selected.)   By Mrs. Gatty.   1s. ⎪
Masterman Ready.   By Capt. Marryat.   (Abgd.)   1s. 6d. ⎬ *Standards IV. & V.*
Settlers in Canada.   By Capt. Marryat.   (Abdg.)   1s. 6d. ⎪
Robinson Crusoe.   1s. 6d. ⎭

Marie; or, Glimpses of Life in France.   By A. R. Ellis. ⎫
  1s. ⎪
Poetry for Boys.   By D. Munro.   1s. ⎪
Southey's Life of Nelson.   (Abridged.)   1s. ⎬ *Standard VI.*
Life of the Duke of Wellington, with Maps and Plans.   1s. ⎪
Gulliver's Travels.   (Abridged.)   [In the press. ⎪
Lamb's Tales.   (Selected.)   [In the press. ⎭

LONDON:
Printed by STRANGEWAYS & SONS, Tower Street, Upper St. Martin's Lane.